Discover
SOUTH AFRICA

Discover
SOUTH AFRICA

PETER JOYCE

First published in 2001 by Struik Publishers
(a division of New Holland Publishing (South Africa) (Pty) Ltd)
London • Cape Town • Sydney • Auckland

86 Edgware Road
W2 2EA London
United Kingdom

14 Aquatic Drive
Frenchs Forest NSW 2086
Australia

80 McKenzie Street
Cape Town 8001
South Africa

218 Lake Road
Northcote, Auckland
New Zealand

Website: www.struik.co.za

10 9 8 7 6 5 4 3 2 1

ISBN 1 86872 518 9

Publishing manager: Annlerie van Rooyen
Managing editor: Lesley Hay-Whitton
Design director: Janice Evans
Designer: Michelle Ludek
Editor: Helen Keevy
Proofreader: Tessa Kennedy
Indexer: Sylvia Grobbelaar
Cartographer: Steven Felmore

Reproduction by Hirt & Carter Cape (Pty) Ltd
Printed in Singapore by Tien Wah Press (Pte) Ltd

PHOTOGRAPHIC CREDITS

Copyright for the photographs rests with Shaen Adey/Struik Image Library with the
exception of the photographs listed below where the copyright rests with the pho-
tographers and/or with their agents as given. [CA = Cape Archives; CLB = Colour
Library; CPJ = Colin Paterson-Jones; DB = David Bristow; DDP = Dennis & de la
Harpe Photography; DR = David Rogers; ET = Erhardt Thiel; GC = Gerald Cubitt;
GD = Gerhard Dreyer; GI = Gallo Images; HvH = Hein von Hörsten; JM = Jackie
Murray; KY= Keith Young; LH = Leonard Hoffmann; LvH = Lanz von Hörsten;
MA = MuseumAfrica; ML = Mark Lewis; MS = Mark Skinner; ND = Nigel Dennis;
PA = Photo Access Photographic Library; PNA = PictureNet Africa; PP = Peter
Pickford; PS = Philip Schedler; RdlH = Roger de la Harpe; SA = Shaen Adey;
SB = Sven Boermeester; SIL = Struik Image Library; SU = Source unknown;
TA = The Argus; TML = The Media Lounge; UWC = UWC/Robben Island Museum/
Mayibuye Archives; WK = Walter Knirr]

Front cover (top left) ML/SIL, (top centre) RdlH/SIL, (top right) ET/SIL, (bottom left)
GD/SIL, (bottom centre) Peter Blackwell/SIL; **half-title** ML/SIL; **imprint page**
RdlH/SIL; **contents** (centre) ML/SIL, (right) PP/SIL; **p. 6** LvH/SIL; **p. 7** (centre)
RdlH/SIL, (right) JM/SIL; **p. 8** (left & right) PP/SIL, (centre) ND/SIL; **p. 12** LvH/SIL;
p. 14 JM/SIL; **p. 15** (bottom) CLB/SIL; **p. 16** ET/SIL; **p. 18** HvH/SIL; **p. 19** (top)
RdlH/SIL, (bottom) KY/SIL; **p. 20** WK/SIL; **p. 21** (bottom) WK/SIL; **p. 22** Benny
Gool/Trace; **p. 22** (left) *Die Burger*, (centre & right) UWC; **p. 24** William Fehr
Collection, The Castle, Cape Town; **p. 25** CA; **p. 26** MA; **p. 29** SU; **p. 30** CA;
p. 31 MA; **p. 32** Barnett Collection; **p. 34** SU; **p. 35** (top) H.W. Wilson New York,
(bottom) MA; **p. 37** CA Repository, ref. No. AG6286; **p. 38** UWC; **p. 39** (left) *The
Star*, (right) SU; **p. 40** Carnegie Commission Reports/ National Archives; **p. 41** (top)
SU, (bottom) Jürgen Schadeberg; **p. 42** Camera Press/Magazine Features;
p. 43 (top) SU, (bottom) TA; **p. 44** Bailey's Archives; **p. 45** Peter Magubane;
p. 46 UWC; **p. 48** Hannes Thiart/TA; **p. 50** Henner Frankenfeld/PNA; **p. 51** João
Silva/PNA; **p. 53** (left) ET/SIL, (centre) JM/SIL, (right) WK/SIL; **p. 54** CLB/SIL;
p. 57 WK; **p. 58** Gerald van Wyk/Koeberg Power Station; **p. 59** Luc Hosten/GI;
p. 60 Ryno/SIL; **p. 61** TA; **p. 64** (left) Jacques Marais/SIL, (top right) DR/SIL, (bottom right) Clinton Whaits/SIL; **p. 65** LvH/SIL; **p. 66** (1) Steve Siebert, (2) WK/SIL,
p. 67 (5) JM/SIL; **p. 68** (1) WK/SIL, (5) SB/TML; **p. 69** (6) *Sunday Times*/GI, (7)
Guy Stubbs/GI, (10) WK/SIL; **p. 70** (1) SB/TML, (2) PS; **p. 71** (5) WK/SIL, (6)
JM/SIL, (7) WK/SIL, (8) JM/SIL, (9) WK; **p. 72** (4) WK; **p. 74** (1) PS, (3&4) WK/SIL;
p. 76 (1) WK/SIL; **p. 77** (2–5) WK/SIL; **p. 78** (4) WK/SIL, (6&8) WK/SIL; **p. 79** (6&8) WK/SIL;
p. 80 (1) WK/SIL; **p. 81** (4) WK/SIL; **p. 82** (1–3) WK/SIL; **p. 83** (4–8) WK/SIL;
p. 84 (1,2&4) Athol Franz Studio, (3) WK/SIL; **p. 85** (5–7) WK/SIL; **p. 86** (1)
WK/SIL, (4) WK; **p. 87** (8&9) HvH/SIL; **p. 88** (1) WK, (2&3) CLB/SIL; **p. 89** (4)
CLB/SIL; **p. 90** (1) LvH/SIL, (3) WK/SIL, (4) RdlH/SIL; **p. 91** (5) LvH/SIL, (7)
RdlH/SIL, (8) WK/SIL; **p. 92** (2&4) WK; **p. 93** (6) WK/SIL, (8) WK, (9)LvH/SIL;
p. 94 (1&2) ND/SIL; **p. 95** (3,4&6) ND/SIL; (5) LvH/SIL; **p. 96** (1&2) LvH/SIL, (3)
Anthony Bannister/GI; **p. 97** (5) LvH/SIL, (6) ND/SIL, (7&8) ND/SIL; **p. 98** (1,4&5)
LvH/SIL; **p. 99** (6) *Getaway*/DR/PA, (7&9) ND/SIL, (8) LvH/SIL; **p. 100** (1) ND/SIL,
(2–4) LvH/SIL; **p. 101** (6,8&9) LvH/SIL; **p. 102** (1&2) WK/SIL; **p. 103** (1–3) WK;
p. 104 (1–3) LvH/SIL; **p. 105** (4) LvH/SIL, (5) DB/PA; **p. 106** (1) WK/SIL, **p. 108**
(1) HvH/SIL, (2) WK/SIL, (3) LvH/SIL, (4) HPH Photography/PA; **p. 109** (5,6&8)
HvH/SIL, (7) LvH/SIL; **p. 110** (1) KY/SIL; **p. 111** (5–7) WK/SIL; **p. 112** (1) WK/SIL;

p. 113 (4) LvH/SIL; **p. 114** (1&2) WK/SIL, (3) ND/SIL; **p. 116** (1) WK/SIL, (2&4)
RdlH/SIL, (3) LvH/SIL; **p. 117** (6) WK/SIL; **p. 118** (1) WK/SIL, (2&3) RdlH/SIL;
p. 119 (5) RdlH/SIL; **p. 120** (1) RdlH/DDP, (2) WK/PA (3&4) RdlH/SIL; **p. 121**
(5&6) RdlH/SIL, (7&8) WK; **p. 122** (2) SA, (5) KY/SIL; **p. 123** (9) RdlH/DDP, (8)
RdlH/SIL; **p. 124** (2) RdlH/SIL; **p. 125** (5,6&7) RdlH/SIL, (8) RdlH/DDP; **p. 126**
(1&3) CLB/SIL, (2) WK/SIL, (4) RdlH/SIL; **p. 127** (5) P. Squire/PA, (6) WK/SIL;
p. 128 (1&2) RdlH/SIL; **p. 129** (5) RdlH/DDP, (6) KY/SIL, (7) RdlH/SIL; **p. 130** (1)
CLB/SIL; **p. 131** (4) KY/SIL, (5) LvH/SIL, (6&7) RdlH/SIL; **p. 132** (1) WK/SIL, (2)
RdlH/SIL; **p. 133** (4) RdlH/SIL, (6) KY/SIL; **p. 134** (1) RdlH/SIL, (2) KY/SIL, (3)
LvH/SIL; **p. 135** (5) WK/SIL, (6) RdlH/SIL, (7) KY/SIL, (8) LvH/SIL; **p. 136** (1)
ND/SIL; **p. 138** (1) KY/SIL, (2) ND/SIL; **p. 140** (1) KY/SIL, (2) ND/SIL, (3)
RdlH/SIL; **p. 141** (4,5&6) ND/SIL, (7&8) RdlH/SIL; **p. 142** (1,2&4) RdlH/SIL;
p. 143 (5) Peter Pinnock; **p. 144** (1,2,3&4) RdlH/SIL; **p. 145** (5,6&8) RdlH/SIL;
p. 146 (1) GPL du Plessis/PA, (2) *Getaway*/DB/PA; **p. 147** (3–6) *Getaway*/DR/PA,
(7) *Getaway*/DB/PA; **p. 148** (1) *Getaway*/DB/PA, (2&3) *Getaway*/ DR/PA; **p. 149**
(4–8) HvH/SIL; **p. 150** (1&2) HvH/SIL, (3) RdlH/SIL; **p. 151** (4) LvH/SIL, (5)
HvH/SIL, (6) RdlH/SIL; **p. 152** (1,2,3&5) HvH/SIL, (4) CPJ; **p. 153** (6) HvH,
(7&10) HvH/SIL, (9) PS; **p. 154** (1–5) HvH/SIL, (7,8&10)
HvH/SIL, (9) KY/SIL; **p. 156** (1) WK/SIL, (2) KY/SIL, (3) HvH/SIL; **p. 157** (6)
PP/SIL, (7) HvH/SIL, (8) ND/SIL; **p. 158** (1) HvH/SIL, (2–4) GD/SIL; **p. 159 &
p. 160** (all) GD/SIL; **p. 161** (5) WK/SIL, (6&7) GD/SIL, (8) MS/SIL; **p. 162** (1)
GD/SIL, (2) PP/SIL, (3) RdlH/DDP; **p. 163** (4,6,7&8) GD/SIL, (5) Leanette Botha;
p. 164–167 (all) GD/SIL; **p. 168** (1) WK/SIL, (3&6) GD/SIL, (4) LvH/SIL;
p. 170 (1) WK/SIL, (2) KY/SIL; **p. 171** (3,4&5) HvH/SIL, (6) WK/SIL; **p. 172** (1)
GD, (3&4) GD/SIL, (2) LvH/SIL; **p. 173** (5&9) HvH/SIL, (6&7) LvH/SIL, (8) WK/SIL;
p. 174 (1) KY, (2) HVH/SIL, (4) PP/SIL, (5) KY/SIL; **p. 175** (8) GD/SIL, (9) LvH/SIL;
p. 176 (1) ET/SIL; **p. 177** (8) ET/SIL; **p. 178** (1) HvH/SIL, (3) LvH/SIL; **p. 179** (4) ET/SIL, (5)
GD/SIL, (6) LvH/SIL; **p. 180** (7) WK; **p. 181** (4&7) ET/SIL, (5) WK, (8) LvH/SIL;
p. 182 (3&4) MS/PA; **p. 183** (5) ET/SIL, (6) LvH/SIL, (7) MS, (8) HvH/SIL;
p. 184 (2) MS/SIL, (3) ET/SIL; **p. 185** (7) ET/SIL; **p. 186** (4) Anthony Johnson/SIL;
p. 187 (7) MS, (8) HvH/SIL; **p. 188** (2) ET/SIL, (3) LvH/SIL; **p. 189** (4) KY/SIL,
(5&7) ET/SIL, (6) WK/SIL; **p. 190** (1) LvH/SIL, **p. 191** (5&7) ET/SIL, (6) LH/SIL,
(8) LvH/SIL; **p. 192** (1&3) HvH/SIL; **p. 193** (5) WK; **p. 194** (1) WK/SIL, (4) ET/SIL;
p. 195 (5) GC, (6) WK; **p. 196** (3) Lionel Soule; **p. 197** (4) MS/PA, (5) LH/SIL, (7)
ET/SIL, (8) CLB/SIL; **p. 198** Monex; **p. 199** (3&7) SA, (4,5&6) KY; **p. 200** (2)
MS/SIL, (3) HvH; **p. 201** (5) HvH/SIL, (6) ET/SIL,(8) HvH/SIL; **p. 202** (1) LvH/SIL,
(3) MS/SIL; **p. 204** (1) HvH/SIL, (2) LvH/SIL, (3) ET/SIL, (4) LvH/SIL; **p. 205** (6,7&9) Craig
Fraser/SIL, (8) MS/SIL; **p. 206** (1) LvH/SIL, (2) HvH/SIL; **p. 207** (4) CLB/SIL,
(5&8) HvH/SIL; **p. 208** (2) GD/SIL, (3) WK/SIL; **p. 209** (6) WK/SIL; **p. 210** (1)
WK/SIL, (3) ET/SIL; **p. 211** (4) WK/SIL, (6) LvH/SIL; **p. 212** (1) LvH/SIL, (3)
GD/SIL; **p. 213** (5) LvH/SIL, (6) GD/SIL; **p. 214** (1) LvH/SIL, (2) Anton Pauw, (3&4)
GD/SIL; **p. 215** (5) LvH/SIL, (6) CPJ; **p. 216** (1,3&4) HvH/SIL, (2) LvH/SIL; **p. 217**
(5) GD/SIL, (6) HvH/SIL, (7) ND/SIL, (8) WK; **p. 218** (1&2) LvH/SIL; **p. 219** (3–5)
LvH/SIL; **p. 220** (1) HvH/SIL, (2) ND/SIL; **p. 221** (3–5) ND/SIL; **p. 222** (1–3)
ND/SIL; **p. 223** (4) KY/SIL, (5–7) CLB/SIL.

Front cover: (*top left*) **Ndebele woman**, (*top centre*) **Zulu beadwork**, (*top right*) **Cape
Point**, (*bottom left*) **Namaqualand**, (*bottom centre*) **leopard**, (*bottom right*) **fruit
vendor**; back cover: **mural in the Newtown Cultural Precinct, Johannesburg** half-title:
girl in front of traditionally decorated Ndebele home; title: **Struisbaai harbour**; imprint
page: **sunflower in the Free State**; contents page: (*left*) **Noordhoek beach**, (*centre*)
Ndebele mural, (*right*) **cheetah fur**.

CONTENTS

  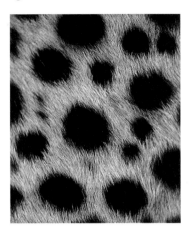

SOUTH AFRICA is a big country: five times the size of Britain, about as large as Holland, Belgium, Italy, France and Germany put together. It stretches from the Limpopo River in the north to blustery Cape Agulhas, nearly 2,000 kilometres to the south, from Namaqualand along the barren western seaboard 1,500 kilometres to subtropical KwaZulu-Natal and the humid Indian Ocean coast: a total land area of just under 1.3 million square kilometres.

Enclosed within South Africa are the separate kingdoms of Lesotho and Swaziland. Far up the Atlantic coastline, beyond the desolate reaches of the Gariep River (until recently known as the Orange), is Namibia, a vast and beautiful country of diamonds, desert and human division that the League of Nations mandated to South Africa after the First World War and which finally gained its independence in 1990. Flanking the Republic's far northern regions are, in clockwise order, the independent states of Botswana, Zimbabwe and Mozambique – a rich territorial diversity.

Indeed, diversity is probably the single word that best illustrates both South and southern Africa. The canvas is kaleidoscopic; variety, contrast and sometimes conflict are vividly evident in the bewildering mix of race and language, creed, colour and culture. The diversity is there, too, in the nature of the land; in its geological formations and regional climates; its mountains, plains and coasts; its rich farmlands, its bushveld scrub and deserts, each of the many different parts supporting its own distinctive plant and animal life. Truly, a world in one country.

In the arid far-western part of the country lies the lonely, hauntingly beautiful Richtersveld (*opposite*), a mountain desert that, despite appearances, is renowned for its plant life. *Above, from left to right*: a Cape Town woman and her fruit and vegetable stall; a Xhosa girl in her traditional finery; and a street barber showing off his capabilities.

PLATEAU AND PLAIN

In physical terms a significant portion of the land is very old. The subcontinent comprises 22 physiographic regions – different geological areas. Some of the rock strata in the valley of the Limpopo and in the Northern Province were formed 4,000 million years ago – not all that long, on the geological calendar, after planet Earth itself began to cool. Others, those belonging to the Kalahari group, are a mere 2 million years old. In between is a score of classifications that, together, tell a large part of the earth's story.

This variety accounts for South Africa's broad-based wealth of mineral resources. The ancient Swazian and Rondian formations, for instance, include gold-bearing reefs that, since their discovery just over a hundred years ago, have transformed the Witwatersrand's quietly rural Highveld into a giant conurbation, recognized for the past half century and more as one of the world's mining and financial capitals. More recently gold, extensive reserves of it, was located in the Free State. Also in the north-central regions, but farther to the west, there are rich

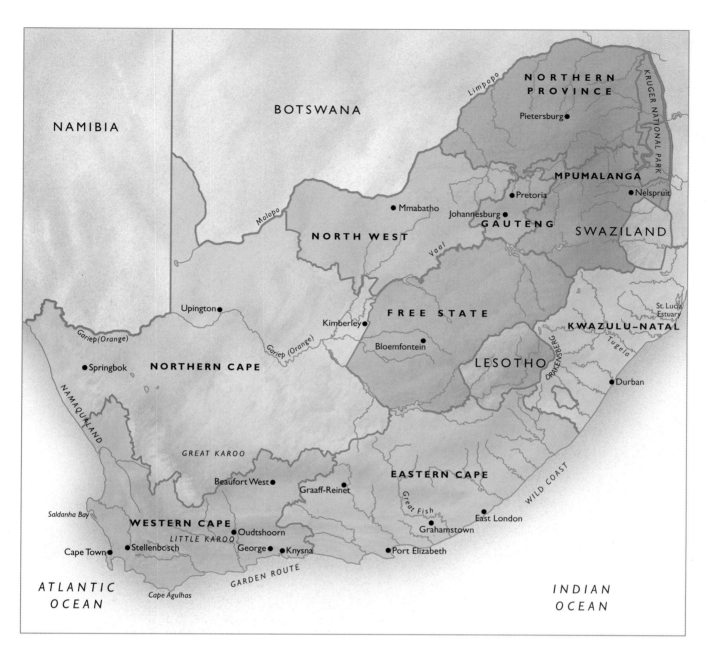

NAMIBIA

BOTSWANA

Limpopo

NORTHERN PROVINCE

Pietersburg •

KRUGER NATIONAL PARK

Molopo

• Mmabatho

MPUMALANGA

• Pretoria

• Nelspruit

Johannesburg •

GAUTENG

NORTH WEST

SWAZILAND

Vaal

Upington •

St. Lucia Estuary

Kimberley •

FREE STATE

KWAZULU–NATAL

Gariep (Orange)

Gariep (Orange)

Bloemfontein •

Tugela

• Springbok

NORTHERN CAPE

LESOTHO

DRAKENSBERG

• Durban

NAMAQUALAND

GREAT KAROO

EASTERN CAPE

WILD COAST

Beaufort West •

Graaff-Reinet •

Great Fish

East London •

Saldanha Bay

Grahamstown •

WESTERN CAPE

• Oudtshoorn

LITTLE KAROO

George • • Knysna

• Port Elizabeth

Cape Town • • Stellenbosch

GARDEN ROUTE

ATLANTIC OCEAN

Cape Agulhas

INDIAN OCEAN

South Africa harbours a wealth of feathered and furry creatures: Cape fur seals are found along the coast (*left*); curious mongooses pop up throughout the country (*centre*); and the cry of the fish eagle echoes across remote watercourses (*right*).

iron and manganese deposits. Platinum and chrome are found in the North West province; coal in the Karoo Sequence; diamonds in the kimberlite pipes of the Northern Cape; copper, zinc, uranium, cobalt, nickel – the list, about 60 commodities in total, extends through almost the entire spectrum of metals and minerals. The only major ingredient that has been lacking is oil, and even this has been discovered off the southern shores.

THE LIE OF THE LAND

If you were to look down on South Africa from an orbiting satellite you would see a clear, quite simple topographical pattern. The land falls into two distinct physical regions: the great interior plateau, semicircular and occupying most of the subcontinent; and the 'marginal zone', which is the relatively narrow coastal and hinterland strip fringing the plateau on three sides. A third, strikingly obvious geographical feature is the division between the two regions: the highly (in the most literal sense) conspicuous and continuous necklace of mountains and hills known as the Great Escarpment.

The plateau is actually the southern tip of the Great African Plateau that rises in the Sahara Desert, some 5,000 kilometres to the north. In southern Africa its altitude varies from the comparatively low 600 metres of the Kalahari Basin to an impressive 3,400 metres in the mountains of Lesotho.

The plateau's rim, the Great Escarpment, begins in the northeast with the craggy Mpumalanga Drakensberg (highest peak Mount Anderson 2,316 metres), then runs southwards, rising in even more splendid grandeur to the famed KwaZulu-Natal Drakensberg's towering faces, some dropping near-vertically 2,000 metres to the plains below. Here are Mont-aux-Sources (3,282 metres); Champagne Castle (3,376 metres); Giant's Castle (3,314 metres); charming and evocative names for some of the most awesome peaks in the southern hemisphere. So formidable is the range that one 250-kilometre stretch may be traversed by just a single, steep route – the Sani Pass.

Southward still, the Escarpment loops inland in a series of smaller ranges: the Stormberg of Anglo-Boer War fame; the Suurberg; the Sneeuberg north of the graceful little Eastern Cape town of Graaff-Reinet. It then disappears into flatland for a while – through this thrust the major surface communications routes between Cape Town and the north – then rises in the impressive granite formations of the Roggeveld and the Kamiesberg range (1,707 metres) and runs on into Namaqualand.

Three hundred million years ago, when the single great landmass called Pangaea first began to succumb to continental drift, slowly, over hundreds of millennia, breaking up to create the global land patterns we know today, the stretch and pull of the earth's crust fashioned the most striking portion of South Africa's marginal zone – the Cape Fold Mountains, which are distinct from the high Escarpment. Legacies of the same mountain-building process are sister ranges in Argentina and in Antarctica.

The series of Cape mountains, running parallel to each other and rising starkly over wide longitudinal valleys, includes the Olifants River, Drakenstein, Hottentots Holland and the splendid Cedarberg ranges in the western parts, and the more intensively folded hills of the Langeberg, Outeniqua, Tsitsikamma and Swartberg in the east, an area that also contains the Little Karoo Basin, 30 by 60 kilometres in extent.

A much larger basin, the wide, shallow, world-famed Great Karoo, extends north from the folded belts. Geologically, the region is a segment of what is known as the Karoo System, which extends over a much wider area. Large parts of it are flat and featureless, though in places the monotony is relieved by dolorite formations – dykes (or ridges) and sills (koppies, or rocky outcrops) – that have been thrust up by millennia of volcanic action and weathered by periodic floods into stark and often bizarre shapes. Perhaps the most remarkable example of this broken country is the jagged jumble of heights known as the Valley of Desolation in the south-east. For the rest, it is a region of far horizons; of the occasional, lonely farmstead girded by its windmill and by the green of willow and gum tree, a brave splash of colour in the immense bleakness; of intense sunshine, blistering days, bitter nights and, always, a great aridness – the very word 'karoo' is derived from a Khoi word meaning 'dry' or 'bare'. Predictably, plant cover is sparse, but special in the way it has evolved and adapted to the harshness: the Karoo's succulents – aloes, crassulas, mesembryanthemums, euphorbias and stapelias – are unique, surviving because they are able to store water in their thick leaves or root systems. And then there are the desert ephemerals, wildflowers whose seeds remain dormant for years, germinating and blooming only when the rare rains come.

WATER IN A DRY LAND

Only a small part of South Africa is blessed by good and regular rains (see page 12). Just a quarter of the country is nurtured by perennial rivers – they flow mainly through the southern coastal belt and from the eastern uplands. There are no real lakes – the large expanse of water called Fundudzi, in the Northern Province, was born of a massive landslide; the tourist-frequented 'lakes' of Zululand and the Knysna-Wilderness district of the southern coastal belt are in reality lagoons. So even the flow of the perennial streams and rivers depends on seasonal and, over long periods, erratic rains. As for the great spaces of the western interior, their riverbeds fill only after the rare summer rainstorms. In South Africa, water is a precious commodity.

Biggest of the river systems is that of the Gariep (formerly the Orange) running westwards from its headwaters in the high Drakensberg for 2,250 kilometres to the Atlantic, plunging magnificently through the granite Augrabies Gorge close to the Namibian border (in exceptional seasons the flow is greater than that of the better known Victoria Falls) before embarking on its last, desolate leg to the sea. Its tributaries include the Caledon and the Vaal, which is actually longer than its big brother but less voluminous.

The Gariep drains almost the entire plateau – 47 per cent of the country. The eastern slopes of the plateau, on the other hand, are comparatively well watered by their small rivers (one of the more substantial is the Letaba, well known to game-viewers in the Kruger National Park). They drain just 12 per cent of the country's surface area but contribute 40 per cent of the run-off. Of the other rivers of the plateau, Kipling's great grey-green Limpopo is the most renowned, demarcating South Africa's northern frontiers with Botswana and Zimbabwe, gathering volume and momentum as it makes its way eastwards to the Indian Ocean north of the Mozambican capital, Maputo. Despite its legend in literature, however, it is not a major river by African standards.

Rural youngsters on their way to the river to fetch water – a precious commodity in most parts of South Africa. Many people outside of the cities have no easy access to clean water supplies.

long – the largest continuous water tunnel in the world.

Even grander in concept and scale is the Lesotho Highlands Water Scheme, one of the most ambitious civil engineering exercises ever undertaken in the southern hemisphere. It is designed eventually (in the second decade of the twenty-first century) to supply the Johannesburg-Pretoria area and its environs with water at a massive rate of 63.6 million cubic metres per second, effectively doubling the annual flow into the Vaal basin, and at the same time to meet all of Lesotho's electrical power needs. The scheme involves the creation of an extensive road network over some of the continent's most rugged terrain, hundreds of kilometres of tunnelling, and a number of the world's largest rock-fill dams.

Significant rivers of the marginal zone include the Sundays and Great Fish, both of which were crucial lines in the often violent territorial disputes between white settlers and black groups in the nineteenth century (*see* page 29); the beautiful Berg River of the Western Cape; and KwaZulu-Natal's Tugela, across which some of the most savage and, for the British, unrewarding battles of the Anglo-Boer War were fought. Supplementary to the river systems are hundreds of pans, or 'floors' – shallow stretches of sometimes salty water (the result of evaporation), biggest of which is the 40 by 64 kilometre Groot Vloer in the Northern Cape.

All told, though, South Africa's rivers do not amount to very much in world terms. Put together, their total run-off is equivalent to that of the Rhine at Rotterdam, and to just half that of the mighty Zambezi 1,000 kilometres to the north.

The country's water resources remain limited and precious; much of the modest volume is lost through spillage, and through evaporation in the intense heat, and there is an ever-increasing demand from the farms, from industry, from the cities, and from rural villagers who have been promised clean and plentiful supplies. Consequently a number of ambitious hydro-engineering projects have been launched, some completed. Among them is the Gariep River Scheme, which accumulates an annual 7,500 million cubic metres of water, irrigates 300,000 hectares of farmland and provides an extra 2,200 million cubic metres for urban use. Its infrastructure includes the huge Gariep and Vanderkloof dams and a system of underground waterways, one of which is 82.5 kilometres

VEGETATION

Colonial settlement of South Africa and the steady encroachment of farmlands and pastures changed the nature of the landscapes and their plant life. Nevertheless, a number of major groups, or vegetation communities, are clearly able to be distinguished.

THE DESERTS AND SEMI-DESERT Excluding the huge and desolate expanses of the Namib, which are not within the Republic's borders, two areas fall into this category. South Africa's only true desert region lies along the western strip of Namaqualand extending into the lower Gariep River valley, a parched region that averages – depending on the precise locality – a scant 50 to 150 millimetres of rainfall a year. In some years there is no rainfall at all. Vegetation is appropriately meagre: a thin ground cover of low, hardy, widely spaced shrubs and succulents and, in springtime, a blaze of bright desert annuals.

One notch higher on the vegetation scale are, first a segment of the Kalahari, which has its dunelands but is more properly classed as arid wilderness, and, second, the Great Karoo (*see* page 9), an enormous area of semi-desert with an uncertain rainfall averaging between 125 and 375 millimetres a year. Again, plant life in the Karoo comprises sparse, tough shrubs and succulents, though grasses occur – and sustain great numbers of sheep where the veld is properly managed – in the more tolerable eastern regions.

THE MEDITERRANEAN (winter-rainfall) areas of the Western Cape. Because of the immense wealth of its plant life, and despite its tiny area, this botanical region is regarded as one of the six floral kingdoms of the world. Forests are found only in the wetter kloofs, but many evergreen shrubs of various heights occur in this region as well as a vast number of indigenous species known collectively as fynbos ('fine bush'). This includes the Cape's famed proteas, ericas, restios and a marvellous diversity of bulbs.

THE BUSHVELD Covering the lower slopes of the central plateau and the Lowveld of eastern Mpumalanga, this area encompasses the great expanse of the Kruger National Park. Flora in the northern parts includes marula and umbrella thorn trees, the elephantine baobab, the fever tree, the ubiquitous dark-green mopane trees and tall tufted grasses. In the more open Kalahari thornbush country, mainly towards the west, there are hardy acacia and camel thorn trees and sparse semi-desert ground cover.

THE TEMPERATE INTERIOR UPLANDS This is the classical veld, consisting of rolling grassy plains and, probably because of winter droughts and frost, few trees – although some exotic species such as willows and eucalyptus (gum trees) thrive.

the monolithic presence of Table Mountain has a profound effect upon local weather conditions: the suburb of Newlands has a much higher rainfall than, for instance, Sea Point; Clifton's sea can be glass-calm while a force four gale blusters over the waters off nearby Milnerton.

THE WEST COAST is a strange, seemingly barren region of rocky, sand-blown shorelines and, stretching inland for anything between 30 and 50 kilometres, terraces of deep, soft, often shifting sand. Dunes are covered by sparse greenery (technically, dwarf bush vegetation), and the land is classed as 'sandveld'. Arid as it looks, though, the western coastal belt has its moment of magic: it is home to some 4,000 floral species, drought-resistant flowering plants which, in springtime, after the life-giving rains and before the onset of the blistering desert breezes, burst into life to transform the countryside into a breathtaking riot of colour. In the far north, around the mouth of the Gariep, the legendary raised beaches are rich with diamonds, swept down by the river over the ages and then distributed by inshore currents.

The west coast sustains much of the country's fishing industry. Here, during the upwelling of the Atlantic waters – usually in spring and summer – rich plant nutrients are carried inshore and

A **STRANGE**, SEEMINGLY BARREN REGION OF **ROCKY, SAND-BLOWN** SHORELINES AND TERRACES OF DEEP, SOFT, SHIFTING SAND

THE SCATTERED FORESTS of the year-round rainfall belt. Once wide-spread but victim to the depredations of man over the centuries, the relics of the marginal zone's great woodlands are now protected by law. Most extensive is the strip, 180 by 16 kilometres, along the southern coast where tall ironwood, yellowwood, stinkwood and other hardwood trees occur. Farther to the north, along the KwaZulu-Natal coast, there are patches of evergreen subtropical tree species, including palms and, in the swampier areas, mangroves.

SEAS AND SHORES

Lapped by two oceans, South Africa's coastline runs 3,000 kilometres from the Atlantic wilderness of the Gariep River mouth in the north-west, round the Cape to northern KwaZulu-Natal and the Mozambican border in the east. Large stretches reward the traveller with spectacular scenery; some are a paradise for the angler, the surfer and the sun-worshipper.

Broadly speaking, the oceans fall into two categories: warm and cooler, the nature of each determined largely by the dominant currents. The warm waters on the east coast emanate from the tropics and flow rapidly south and south-west as the Agulhas Current, which more or less hugs the coast until, near Cape Agulhas, it turns south and east. Along the west coast, the main waterbody comes from the South Atlantic as the north-flowing Benguela Current, and is much cooler.

Because of the configuration of the coast around the Cape Peninsula and the prevailing wind patterns, the water temperatures between False Bay and Table Bay can differ by as much as 12°C during the summer. Indeed, the Cape Peninsula is full of contrasts. Apart from the 'two-oceans' syndrome,

Much of the wild, wind-swept western coastal region has a haunting beauty all of its own.

the plankton, basic to the area's rich stocks of mussels, thrives. These shellfish are primary feeders, and in their turn they support massive populations of rock lobsters (crayfish), snoek, stockfish (Cape hake) and, at times, tunny, marlin and yellowtail.

The Hole-in-the-Wall, a detached cliff with an arched opening, is among the most distinctive features of the Wild Coast.

THE SOUTH AND EAST COASTS are much more heavily populated and, in tourist terms, more popular. In the south, one stretch of shoreline with its hinterland is especially beautiful: the 220-kilometre Garden Route that extends roughly from Mossel Bay in the west to the Tsitsikamma Forest and Storms River in the east. This is a green and flowered region of charming bays and beaches, cliffs and pounding surf overlooked by the not-too-distant and quite splendid Outeniqua and Tsitsikamma mountains. Equally enticing to holidaymakers are the coasts north and south of Durban in the east: wide, dune-backed sandy strips fringing a remarkably straight shoreline (Durban itself, with its Point and 16-kilometre-long Bluff embracing a lagoon-type bay, is something of an exception).

In fact, there are precious few good natural harbours along the entire length of the Republic's coastline – Saldanha Bay is the best, but it was passed over by the early seafarers in favour of the more exposed but better watered Table Bay. It is generally an even coastline, without many pronounced embayments, and most of the otherwise suitable estuaries are inhibited by sandbars, the product of currents and the heavy sediment brought by rivers with steep gradients and sporadic flow. East London, in the Eastern Cape, is the country's only river port and its harbour, on the Buffalo River, is subject to constant dredging operations. Durban's sandbar is particularly notorious. The city's port is one of the hemisphere's biggest and busiest, but it was only in 1892, after decades of frustrating experiments with breakwaters and sand-pumps, that the 2,820-ton *Dunrobin Castle* managed to sail into harbour – the first ocean-going liner to do so.

CLIMATE

Weather patterns, influenced by different ocean currents, by altitude and prevailing winds and by the ever-changing nature of the land, are subject to sharp regional variation. Climatically, South Africa could be half a dozen entirely separate countries.

When it comes to rainfall, however, there are three broad but distinct regions. The south-western tip of the subcontinent, centring round the lovely city of Cape Town, has winter precipitation; the southern and eastern coastal belts enjoy (in good years) perennial showers which are heavy, almost tropical in KwaZulu-Natal. Rains over the rest of the country – on the great central plateau and towards the east – come with sudden summer thunderstorms that are brought by north-easterly winds.

This is not to say that the land, as a whole, is well watered. On the contrary, South Africa is one of the world's drier countries: mean annual rainfall is little over 460 millimetres compared with a global average of 857 millimetres. The rains, too, tend to be unpredictable; drought has been the norm rather than the exception in recent times. And the farther west one goes the less generous the heavens are (with the exception of the south-western Cape): along the shores of the Indian Ocean and in the KwaZulu-Natal hinterland a healthy 1,000 millimetres of rain can be expected to fall each year; in the western extremities of the country the average tends to be around 200 millimetres, and some of the thirstlands are lucky if they get a meagre 50 millimetres.

Average annual temperatures are more constant. The northern areas are not, as one might perhaps expect, very much hotter than the southern because the land rises to the high central plateau, which is generally cooler than other parts of the world lying within the same lines of latitude. Cape Town can be suffocating and its annual average temperature is 17°C; Pretoria, a full 1,500 kilometres nearer the tropics, can freeze and its annual average is only half a degree more. But again, air temperatures in the east are generally higher than those in the western coastal regions, affected respectively by the warm Agulhas and the cold Benguela currents. Temperature inversions also vary quite dramatically from place to place. They are least at the coast and greatest in the interior, where clear-skied winter nights are bitterly cold while the days remain sunny and mild.

South Africa, in fact, is blessed with a great deal of sunshine, the average number of cloud-free hours a day varying (depending on the area) from about 7.5 to 9.4 compared with New York's 6.9, Rome's 6.4 and London's 3.8 hours of sunshine a day. Some parts of the country, the dust-dry western districts, for instance, register a bare 10 or so overcast days a year.

The climate of the interior, in the rising lands beyond the Escarpment, is fairly uniform: bone-dry, sunny winters; summer days (from about November to February) of mounting storm clouds and late-afternoon downpours. At least, that is the traditional pattern in the north-central and eastern parts, where, apart from Kimberley in the Northern Cape, the inland cities and most of the towns are situated.

The climates of the different seaboard regions are more variable and interesting. The south-western part of the Western Cape – Cape Town, the Peninsula, its coastal extensions and hinterland – is unique within the southern African context in its Mediterranean character. It has dry summers with long, cloudless days which are sometimes – in what are called 'berg wind conditions' (hot air blowing in from the northern interior) – perfect in their somnolent stillness, at other times disturbed by a gusty, unnerving south-easter that often reaches gale force and can last for up to a week or more. In winter it is wet and cool – downright cold at times; snow falls on the surrounding mountains. The best Cape months are those of its brief spring (September and October) and autumn (March and April) when colours are changing and the fragile delicacy of the air lifts and sustains the spirit.

Northwards, up the Namaqualand coastal districts, the climate becomes even drier and hotter until you eventually get to the Gariep River and the endless, waterless tracts of the Namib Desert. As mentioned, though, springtime in Namaqualand is a spectacularly flamboyant affair: for a few brief weeks the barren desert countryside is covered by multicoloured carpets of small, exquisite flowers.

Along the other coast, stretching east to Port Elizabeth, the climate changes from Mediterranean to temperate. Again the summers are warm (and windy); the winters cool. Here there is rainfall all year round – or there should be: the Eastern Cape, like most of the rest of the country, has at times suffered crippling droughts. Following the Indian Ocean coastline as it inclines northwards, one enters the subtropical region of KwaZulu-Natal, where it is hot and stickily humid in summer (though the uplands are cooler and very pleasant), chilly to warm in winter, and rainy throughout, but wetter during the summer months.

THE PEOPLE

South Africa has an estimated population of around 41 million. One cannot be more exact because although censuses are periodically taken they are soon outdated, and the very nature of society and the mobility of some of its elements have made it difficult, if not impossible, to paint a precise statistical picture. Of the four major ethnic groups, black people number approximately 31 million, whites nearly 5 million, those of Asian origin around a million and the coloured (mixed-descent) community between 3 and 4 million.

Growth rates vary quite sharply among groups – predictably, since South Africa is anything but homogeneous. Most black people have their roots in the countryside. They come from a background of subsistence farming, their communities traditionally structured. Cultural taboos and perceived economic necessity inhibit family planning: the extended family is an accepted and effective form of social security. Southern Africa is no different from the rest of the world: the poorer, less educated tend to have large families. With greater urbanization and higher standards of living, a decline in the birth rate can be expected, a decline accelerated by the onslaught of the AIDS pandemic, which is already making tragic inroads into the country's human landscape.

A crucial feature of the past few decades has been urban drift, the migration of people – especially black people – from the countryside to the cities. Industrial expansion since the Second World War has meant jobs, or at least the prospect of jobs, in and around the major centres: an irresistible lure to the hundreds of thousands who would otherwise have to scratch a meagre living from the soil in areas that are not favoured by many modern amenities, and where, because of 'separate development' and consequent overcrowding, overstocking and erosion, much of the land is poor and becoming even poorer. With the dismantling of apartheid and its 'group areas' and 'influx control' restrictions, the rate of urbanization has increased dramatically. In the 1990s it was estimated that 700,000 people were abandoning the rural life each year.

Biggest of the country's conurbations is the Pretoria-Johannesburg axis and its satellites – South Africa's industrial heartland. This immense cluster of concrete nuclei, each ringed by its dormitory suburbs, has a population of some 8 million people; it covers less than 1 per cent of the country's land area but is home to about a fifth of its inhabitants. Soweto – acronym for South-Western Townships – started life as a collection of 'locations' housing 'temporary' labour for Johannesburg's gold mines. It is now a city in its own right, one of around 2 million souls (that is the official figure; in reality it probably accommodates a great many more), and its commuters include highly qualified people – artisans, executives, professionals – as well as miners, labourers, the self-employed and the unemployed. Other centres – Cape Town, Port Elizabeth, Durban-Pinetown – have grown in a similar fashion if rather less spectacularly.

Whatever the strains it imposes, though, mass-migration to the cities is now regarded not so much as a problem as a natural, unstoppable process that could in fact help alleviate some of the country's most worrying ailments. Badly needed infrastructural, social and other services, for instance, can be more easily and cheaply created for large concentrations of people than for widely scattered rural populations. Such apartheid-era endeavours as decentralization and influx control proved enormously costly in terms of money, social relations and human dignity, and they failed dismally. The new freedom of movement will indeed lead to the creation of huge urban communities, but it is easier to provide people with jobs, with houses and clinics and schools, electric lighting, proper sanitation and all the other ingredients of a decent life if they are close to and part of the established centres. Moreover, quite apart from their potential as reservoirs of manpower, technical skills and professional expertise, large urban concentrations – the recently structured mega-cities or 'unicities' – have a habit of becoming economically self-generative, indeed of functioning more coherently in the global marketplace than the provincial and even the national body economic.

Increasingly, as political freedom opens the doors to social democracy in the new South Africa, it will become possible to write about the people without qualification along racial lines. But today's reality is that the racial groups have not shared a common heritage and are not, for reasons of history, of past regulation and in some cases of choice, fully integrated. Any objective summary of the diverse population must therefore take account of the separate identities.

THE BLACK PEOPLE Although there are close historical and cultural affinities, the black people of southern Africa do have their separate cultural identities: they are distinguished by custom, social system and language into a number of groupings. The divisions are not clearly evident in the party-political arena nor in the context of increasingly detribalized urban life, but in other respects the principal black groups can be regarded as distinctive societies. They comprise the Zulu, the Xhosa, the Swazi (all three are related, belonging to the Nguni group of people); the Northern Sotho (Bapedi), the Southern Sotho (Basotho) and the Tswana (the Tswana are the western branch of the Sotho); the South Ndebele and the North Ndebele; the Venda; and the Shangaan-Tsonga.

The ways of the countryside are still apparent in town and city but, with massive urbanization, traditions are rapidly disintegrating.

This cultural mosaic might suggest that South Africa's black communities have clung tenaciously to traditional African ways and remain outside the mainstream of western influence, which of course is patently not so. Custom, tradition and ancient loyalties do persist, most obviously, but not exclusively, in the rural areas. They are enshrined, for instance, in the rules of courtship and marriage; in matters of inheritance, guardianship and seniority within the clan; in kinship bonds, the social order and the spiritual force of ancestry; in the assumptions underlying land tenure; and in concepts of wealth.

The heritage is also there in more obvious, more visible forms. Wander off the beaten track in Zululand and you will see, here and there, beautifully crafted 'beehive' homes and, occasionally, the plumed and feathered ceremonial regalia of an earlier and perhaps more romantic age. Some Ndebele women decorate their houses in strikingly colourful geometric patterns and a few of them still wear tight, multi-ringed anklets, armlets and necklaces that can never be removed. Venda girls perform the sinuous *domba* snake-dance on their journey into womanhood. The Swazi of the KaNgwane region honour their ancestors and their chiefs, affirm their nationhood and celebrate the first fruits of the soil in an exuberant, week-long festival called the Great Incwala. Xhosa folk of both sexes smoke long wooden pipes, the women fashion beadwork of stunning intricacy and subtle meaning, their teenage sons undergo painful (and hazardous) circumcision rituals.

That is the old Africa. The new co-exists (often uncomfortably) and may in due course supercede. Many of the millions of urban black people are second and third generation townspeople; hundreds of thousands are migrant workers; all have been dramatically exposed to the blessings and curses of the acquisitive society. The traditional order, in the towns, has been largely eroded, to be replaced by a transitional but distinct subculture that encompasses (engulfs, in many tragic instances) everything from social structure and family life to music, literature and language.

Whether urbanization, and its multiple assaults on African tradition, is a good or bad thing remains a complex issue, the conclusion subjective. What is no longer open to question, though, is the inevitability of a radically changed human landscape.

THE ASIAN PEOPLE A need for labour to harvest the crops of the Natal Colony's new and vast sugar plantations in the mid-nineteenth century prompted the importation of thousands of workers from India. They were indentured (contracted) for between three and five years, after which they had the choices of repatriation, of renewing their contracts, or of accepting Crown land and remaining as settlers. Most took up the land option.

The first shipload disembarked in Durban 1860. They were joined by non-indentured 'passenger' immigrants from the Indian subcontinent – British subjects able to travel freely within the Empire, and choosing Natal as their home. Today, South Africa's Asian community numbers some 900,000, most of whom – 85 per cent – live in and around the Durban-Pinetown complex. Nearly all the remainder, about 100,000 people, are settled in Gauteng.

The Indian society, generally a prosperous one, has its own distinct traditions, underpinned by religion and by *kutum* – the disciplined, patriarchal extended family which regulates relationships and social interaction. The community is remarkably unified but also organized according to faith – Hindu and Muslim. The Hindu element is in turn divided into four language groups (Tamil, Telegu, Hindustani and Gujarati) and subscribes to its own fairly strict rules governing manners, rituals, food and drink. The Muslims come from a linguistic background of Gujarati and Urdu, and observe precisely defined codes of belief and behaviour.

Again, though, traditions are being eroded, especially among the younger generation. The sari and other traditional Indian garments

The hour of prayer in one of South Africa's numerous mosques.

are giving way, if not always to T-shirts and jeans, certainly to the more conservative Western style of dress; there is movement towards the smaller family; traditional male authority no longer goes unquestioned; young Indian women lead far freer and more diverse lives than their mothers and grandmothers; and English is by and large the chosen means of communication. Always a significant component of the South African economy – the community has an exceptionally high proportion of professionals and entrepreneurs – the Indians only recently attained full political rights. They were, though, the first to challenge both prejudice and formal discrimination. The Natal Indian Congress was formed in 1894 by Mohandas Gandhi, the Mahatma ('Great Soul'), and, under his leadership and inspiration, conducted courageous and partially successful 'passive resistance' campaigns between 1906 and 1914. The organization gave birth to the Transvaal Indian Congress and, in 1920, to the nationwide South African Indian Congress (SAIC). The SAIC remained a moderate pressure group until the passage of the 1946 Asiatic Land Tenure Act (which, among other things, placed severe limitations on Indian ownership and occupation of land), but thereafter it became increasingly militant. In 1949 it allied itself with the African National Congress, and in 1954 formally endorsed the watershed Freedom Charter, manifesto of the most powerful of the South African liberation movements.

THE COLOURED PEOPLE The country's 3 million-strong coloured community, the majority of whom live in the Western Cape, has diverse origins. The early Dutch settlers imported slaves from Holland's Eastern possessions, from elsewhere in Africa and from some of the islands of the Atlantic and Indian oceans, and admixtures steadily and inevitably followed, Khoisan, Xhosa and whites adding their own progeny over the decades.

Significant subgroups include the Griquas of the north-eastern and north-western regions, the product of European-

Youngsters keep themselves entertained at Arniston near Cape Agulhas, the southernmost tip of the African continent.

Khoisan miscegenation; the coloured people of KwaZulu-Natal, many of whom trace their ancestry to immigrants from Mauritius and St Helena; and the 200,000 Muslims of the Cape Peninsula, a close-knit society that has maintained its strict Islamic ways over the centuries since their forebears arrived from Indonesia, Madagascar, Ceylon (now Sri Lanka) and China.

In general terms, though, the coloured people of South Africa are culturally very much part of the western world. Some 87 per cent are of the Christian faith; the majority speak Afrikaans; and they are barely separable in lifestyle, social organization and aspiration from people of exclusively European origin.

Before apartheid, in fact, the coloured people were more or less an integrated part of the Cape community as a whole, enjoying, among other things, the constitutionally entrenched common-roll franchise – until it was removed in the 1950s. Under apartheid they were subject to a special classification. Coloured residential areas were delineated; the famed District Six, close to the heart of Cape Town, was demolished in the late 1970s and early 1980s and most of its inhabitants moved to huge, new and some-what characterless townships such as Mitchell's Plain on the windblown Cape Flats. The move was bitterly resented and for years the site of District Six remained undeveloped, a scar on Cape Town's land-scape and on the minds of its citizens.

Whatever the indignities suffered, how-ever, the coloured community has remained a resilient one with, among other things, a surprisingly exuberant musical tradition of its own. The origins of the banjo-accompanied Cape 'goemaliedjie' songs are obscure, though they do owe something to the American Deep South. The cheerful, often racy words and melodies are still heard at such gatherings as the New Year festival, when brightly dressed minstrel troupes bring joy and colour to the streets of Cape Town.

THE WHITE PEOPLE For much of the twentieth century South Africa had two official languages (there are now 11, though English is inexorably gaining favour as the principal means of communication), reflecting the dual origins of what were for long the country's politically dominant cultural groups.

The Afrikaners are descendants of the early Cape Dutch settlers and of people of other nationalities who they absorbed. Today they number something over 2.5 million people. High Dutch was the stem from which Afrikaans branched, taking on new words and a different shape over three centuries of isolation from the original homeland and, later, also from the principal Cape settlement.

The German and French elements are significant (and, linguis-tically, the black languages as well): the Afrikaners in fact have a rich mix of cultures in their blood, one official estimate pegging the ancestral ingredients at only 40 per cent Dutch; a surprising

40 per cent German; 7.5 per cent British (mainly Scots); 7.5 per cent French and 5 per cent others. The French connection, through the hardy Protestant Huguenots who fled Europe in the 1680s, can be discerned in surnames such as du Plessis, du Toit and Marais; the Dutch in the 'van' prefixes. Curiously, there seems to be very little that is clearly German in language, custom or nomenclature. Their assimilation appears to have been total. Over the decades, the Afrikaner community expanded from its very small beginnings in the Cape, more as a consequence of natural increase than from immigration (hence the proliferation of certain names – Botha, Malan, and so on).

A busker entertains passers-by in Cape Town's busy centre. Young white South Africans no longer have automatic access to jobs in the formal economy; something that was almost guaranteed under apartheid.

Families have always tended to be large, patriarchal, Calvinistic and close-knit; groups of families clannish – the universal charac-teristics of pioneer people.

Despite the mixture of antecedents, and despite bouts of bitter factionalism, the story of the Afrikaner has been one of fierce pride in nation, of unity under threat, and of tough and uncompromising cultural exclusivity. All of which is understandable enough: the early settlers, especially those of the eastern Cape Colony, found plenty of lonely hardship in a land made inhospitable by the elements, natural hazard and violence, and came to trust for survival in musket, Bible and the closing of ranks.

Then, with the establishment of British rule at the beginning of the nineteenth century, came greater bureaucratic control, a degree of deprivation and a threat to their identity. So in the late 1830s they inspanned their ox-wagons and trekked into the great northern wilderness in search of peace, living-space and the right to pursue their own lives unmolested, none of which they found in lasting measure. Fabulous deposits of gold were located beneath the pastoral surface of their Promised Land;

foreigners flocked into the fledgling Boer states that they had established and once again the Afrikaners felt themselves besieged, a fear that was brutally confirmed by the Jameson Raid of 1895–96 and the cynical diplomatic prelude to full-scale war three years later (*see page 35*).

In short, from their early settler years, Afrikaners saw themselves as a hounded and beleaguered people – and with some justice. It was only towards the middle of the twentieth century that Afrikanerdom – not the bridge-building kind of Louis Botha and Smuts but the uncompromising, rather xenophobic Afrikanerdom of J.B.M. Hertzog, D.F. Malan and H.F. Verwoerd – could challenge English-speaking South Africans for economic and political dominance.

This, put briefly and perhaps simplistically, is the historical legacy. The heirs to it, in extremely broad terms, fall into two groups: those who have come to terms with the new order and play a full part in the forging of a united nation; and a fast-diminishing conservative element who still think much as their forebears did. The latter, being driven by an age-old fear of the 'black tide', favour isolation within a *Volkstaat*, or Afrikaner people's republic.

South Africa is home to just under 2 million English-speaking whites, and their legacy is entirely different from that of the Afrikaners. Their background is colonial rather than pioneer; urban-industrial rather than rural.

There were half a dozen watershed events (which are covered in more detail in *The Past*, page 23) in the history of the English-speaking settlement in South Africa.

First was the British occupation of the Cape (technically, two occupations: the inaugural one between 1795 and 1803, and the second from 1806 onwards) during the French revolutionary and Napoleonic wars, when the landing of the redcoats ended over a century of Dutch East India Company rule and ushered in an era of deliberate 'anglicization'. Part of this process was the second major influx: the arrival of 4,000 or so British settlers at Algoa Bay in the eastern Cape Colony in 1820. Farther east, the colonization of Natal – a more independently motivated exercise – gathered momentum from the 1840s with a series of privately organized immigration schemes.

The fourth, essentially two-pronged British onslaught, was the birth of South Africa's huge mining industry with the discovery of diamonds in the northern Cape Colony (near present-day Kimberley) in 1867 and the accidental discovery (by two casual labourers) of gold on the Transvaal's Witwatersrand in 1886. These drew large numbers of *uitlanders* ('outlanders', or foreigners) to the northern areas, most of whom were English-speaking. Much later, further large migrations occurred after the Second World War and, in the post-colonial era, with the granting of independence to Britain's East African territories and Zambia, which produced a trickle of immigrants. Recent years have witnessed the slow, convulsive demise of unilaterally independent white Rhodesia (now Zimbabwe), which prompted something of a flood.

The strongholds of the present English-speaking community were thus historically determined. It is no accident that South Africa's 'English' universities are in Cape Town (UCT), Grahamstown (Rhodes University), in KwaZulu-Natal (Durban and Pietermaritzburg) and Johannesburg (the University of the Witwatersrand). Other than the significant English-speaking farming communities established in the Eastern Cape and in the sugar and fruit-growing regions of KwaZulu-Natal, it is very largely an urban community.

Traces of the colonial psychology persisted until well after the Second World War. In affluent homes along the gracious tree-lined avenues of Constantia in the Cape and in Pietermaritzburg people would speak, in accents indistinguishable from those of upper-middle-class Surrey and Sussex, of England as 'home', toast the Queen on her birthday and eat plum pudding in the midday heat of a southern Christmas. But these now represent very much an anachronistic minority. Most English-speaking South Africans have long since detached themselves from their ancestral origins and identify wholly with the country, although some do tend to drift away, many of them to Britain.

Until fairly recently, too, the English-speaking section had a virtual monopoly on the non-agrarian economy; the reins of commerce and industry were firmly in Anglo-Saxon and Jewish hands. This is no longer the case. Even before Afrikanerdom assumed control of central government and the bureaucracy in 1948 it was flexing its economic muscles. Today, despite rapid black empowerment, substantial segments of the private sector are run by Afrikaans-speakers.

A number of smaller ethnic and linguistic groups make up the residue of the white community. Most substantial – estimates vary widely but there are probably about 75,000 – are South Africans of Portuguese extraction, most of them former residents of Lisbon's southern African territories of Mozambique and Angola, though a substantial number hail from the small Atlantic island of Madeira.

A significant subgroup of English-speaking South Africans are the Jewish people, comprising about 2.5 per cent of the white population. Though relatively small in numbers, Jewish South Africans have contributed markedly to the business and industrial development of the country: personalities of the past such as Barney Barnato, Lionel Phillips, Samuel Marks and Alfred and Otto Beit played prominent parts in the early days of the diamond- and goldfields. In the world of the arts, both performing and visual and in literature, so many Jews have distinguished themselves that it would be invidious to single out any name.

WHERE THE PEOPLE LIVE

In 1910 the Crown colonies of Natal and the Cape of Good Hope and the former Boer republics of the Transvaal and the Orange Free State were brought together as provinces of the Union of South Africa. This territorial structure lasted until 1994, when the country was divided up into nine provincial regions in terms of the new quasi-federal arrangement, and the former black 'homelands' – four independent republics and six self-governing national states – were reincorporated.

THE PROVINCES

The nine provincial divisions, each with their own premier, parliament and civil service, enjoy a certain degree of legislative and administrative autonomy (*see page 53*). Briefly, the nine provinces are:

WESTERN CAPE The oldest, most populous and economically advanced segment of the old Cape Province. The new region embraces Cape Town and the Peninsula; a beautiful hinterland of mountains and valleys rich in vineyards, orchards and pastures; approximately half (the more fertile half) of the country's western seaboard; the lovely south coast (this stretch known as the Garden Route) as far as Plettenberg Bay, and a fairly large expanse of the semi-arid Great Karoo. Capital: Cape Town. Population: 6.7 million.

EASTERN CAPE A large, heavily populated and unevenly developed region that takes in the coastal city of Port Elizabeth and its surrounding 'settler country' and the former independent republics of Transkei and Ciskei. The major growth areas are Port Elizabeth-Uitenhage and East London-King William's Town-Bisho. Capital: Bisho. Population: 6.3 million.

NORTHERN CAPE The largest region in geographical terms – it covers 30 per cent of South Africa, stretching from the Namaqualand seaboard in the west to the Kimberley diamond-fields in the north-central part of the country

The snow-mantled plains of the Free State. This is a rare sight in the province where summer days can be blistering.

– but also the most sparsely populated and least developed. Much of the terrain is covered by the dry sands of the Karoo and, in the far north, the Kalahari. Capital: Kimberley. Population: a little less than 850,000.

KWAZULU-NATAL The region corresponds, with minor adjustments, to the old Natal province and the KwaZulu homeland it incorporated, and it supports the largest of the regional populations: nearly 9 million people are crowded into the 92,000 square kilometres that lie between the grandness of the Drakensberg and the warm waters of the Indian Ocean. Capital: Pietermaritzburg and Ulundi were vying for capital status at the time of writing. Population: 9 million.

FREE STATE This province, on the high, mostly open plains of the central plateau, occupies about a tenth of South Africa's land area, yields a third of its maize and wheat harvests and sustains 80 per cent of its sheep and a substantial percentage of the national cattle population. Mining output includes gold, diamonds, platinum and coal. Capital: Bloemfontein. Population: nearly 3 million.

NORTH WEST This province comprises the former western Transvaal and part of the former northern Cape, and is something of a Cinderella region. It has its platinum, chrome and other mines (around Rustenburg and Klerksdorp) but the regional economy is increasingly dependent on farming: fruit, vegetables and flowers around the beautiful Magaliesberg hills, great fields of golden maize elsewhere. The province encompasses most of the former republic of Bophuthatswana and the tourist playground of Sun City and the sparkling attraction of the Lost City. It also includes the popular Pilanesberg National Park. Capital: Mmabatho. Population: just over 3.5 million.

NORTHERN PROVINCE A region of bushveld, rich grasslands and enchanting hills (notably the Waterberg and, near the Limpopo River, the Soutpansberg). There are no major growth points – the Pietersburg area, its largest centre, accounts for just 0.6 per cent of the country's employment – and the province lags far behind the field in the development stakes. Its tourism potential, though, is excellent: among other things it encompasses half the Kruger National Park, and the Waterberg is growing increasingly popular. Capital: Pietersburg. Population: 5 million.

and judiciary. A powerful body of northern politicians, however, now wants to confer comprehensive capital status on Pretoria, a move strenuously opposed by Capetonians. The debate is likely to continue, acrimoniously, for years, and it could prove highly divisive. South Africa's principal urban centres, in order of age, are:

CAPE TOWN which had its beginnings in 1652 with the landing of Jan van Riebeeck and his small party of settlers. Greater Cape Town, which sprawls over much of the Peninsula and northwards up the western seaboard to Atlantis, is home to a large coloured community, a rapidly growing black population which is now thought to exceed a million, and to around half a million white residents. The city's setting, beneath and around the moody grandeur of Table Mountain, is without doubt one of the loveliest in the southern hemisphere. Cape Town's port is quieter than it was in the heyday of the passenger steamer (other harbours, closer to the northern industrial markets, have poached much of its freight traffic), but marine and mercantile enterprises still contribute substantially to the local economy. The city's wider base includes light engineering and manufacturing, the service industries and tourism – the beaches, the attractive wineland-and-mountain hinterland, the historical legacy, the calendar of arts, the eating and drinking places, the undemanding, unhurried lifestyle, are all powerful attractions. A great many people retire to or near the city.

Orange Barberton daisies grace the Mpumalanga landscape; the province's eastern parts are a scenic delight.

MPUMALANGA The second smallest region (it was formerly known as Eastern Transvaal) with the fastest growing economy, much of the impetus provided by planned development within and around the 'Maputo Corridor' linking the region with neighbouring Mozambique. Industry is currently concentrated around the mining centres of Witbank and Middelburg on the Highveld plateau to the west; in the east are the splendid mountains of the Mpumalanga Drakensberg and, beyond, the subtropical abundance of the fertile and beautiful Crocodile River Valley, the heat-hazed, game-rich Lowveld plain and the Kruger National Park. Capital: Nelspruit. Population: about 3 million.

GAUTENG The province, the smallest of all in area, encompasses the cities of Pretoria and Johannesburg together with the complex centred on Vereeniging to the south. Gauteng is both densely populated and rich: around 370 people are crammed into each of its 1,900 square kilometres, and it generates around 40 per cent of the gross national product. It originally drew its wealth from the gold mines of the Witwatersrand but now boasts a hugely diverse industrial economy (see further on). Capital: Johannesburg. Population: around 7 million.

Cape Town's Chapman's Peak Drive, though plagued by rock-falls, and at times partially closed, ranks among the country's finest scenic routes. It leads eventually to Cape Point.

THE MAIN CENTRES

Since Union in 1910 the country has had three capital cities: to propitiate the most important of the rival regional interests the Union negotiators settled on Cape Town, Pretoria and Bloemfontein as the respective seats of the legislature, administration

PORT ELIZABETH It is difficult to say with certainty whether Port Elizabeth or Durban is South Africa's second-oldest city. Probably Port Elizabeth, which is where the British settlers of 1820 set their optimistic feet ashore (*see* page 29). It is now a sprawling modern city of dockyards, motor assembly plants, factories and commercial buildings sustaining, together with its satellites of Uitenhage and Kirkwood, some half a million economically active people. Port Elizabeth was especially hard hit by the recessions of the mid-1980s and early 1990s. Not far away is historic Grahamstown, familiarly known as the 'city of saints' because of its many churches, and officially a city because of the presence of its small cathedral. Overlooked by Monument Hill, home to Rhodes University, several famous schools and to the National Arts Festival, Grahamstown, keeper of English South Africa's soul, is among the most attractive of the country's smaller centres.

It is still doing so: Greater Durban is said to be the world's fastest-growing urban conglomeration, its population expanding faster than those of Calcutta and Mexico City, but expanding for much the same reasons. The armies of the poor have been leaving a countryside that can no longer meet their minimum needs, and are congregating in their thousands around KwaMashu, Ntujuma, Umlazi, Embumbula and other ramshackle settlements on the northern and western city fringes. Their integration into the urban mainstream, the provision of jobs, houses, schools, clinics – these are Durban's real priorities, and the contrast between the reality

Fishermen haul their nets across Durban's beach; the city's ultra-modern seafront provides an incongruous backdrop.

DURBAN, on the KwaZulu-Natal coast and third largest of the country's cities – and its largest port – is aptly known as 'South Africa's playground'. Durban is not, however, the provincial capital: that honour belongs, tenuously (Ulundi is vying for capital status) to the pretty little city of Pietermaritzburg some 90 kilometres inland.

Durban is now very much an African city, but its origins and its history, are very English. It started life as the trading and white-hunter outpost of Port Natal when, in 1824, Lieutenant Farewell of the good ship *Julia* (he had previously served on the *Beagle* of Darwinian fame) disembarked with 40 white settlers, to whom the Zulu king Shaka, with surprising benevolence, granted 900 square kilometres of rich land around the bay. Progress was slow at first (in 1835 there were still only 30 or so residents), but with the launching of private immigration schemes in the 1840s and, later, the dredging of the harbour entrance, the town expanded rapidly.

and the image the city projects, that of a playground for the privileged, is marked indeed. But then it is only by exploiting its considerable natural assets to the full, by offering the ultimate in frivolous pleasure, that Durban can remain prosperous enough to cope with the future.

Greater Durban is also home to large numbers of Indian people, many of them direct descendants of the indentured labourers brought in during the 1860s to work the great sugar plantations of the region (*see* page 14).

BLOEMFONTEIN, capital of the Free State and judicial capital of the Republic, sprawls over 16,900 hectares of dry, treeless central plateau countryside. It is largely an administrative city (though it has 350 or so light industries, and the largest railway workshops in the country) – around 40 per cent of its economically active citizens are employed in social, community or government services. The town has some fine buildings, notably the nineteenth-century republican Raadsaal, or parliament, a dignified mix of Renaissance form and Classical-revival detail, and a splendid new Opera House that was completed in 1985.

Pretoria, known as the 'Jacaranda City', is graced by an unusual number of attractive parks and gardens.

PRETORIA, state administrative capital and a place of some one million souls, is known as the 'Jacaranda City' because of the 7,000 or so lovely lilac-blossomed trees that grace its gardens, parks and about 650 kilometres of well-laid-out streets. The city has a magnificent setting, overlooked by hills on which the renowned architect Herbert Baker placed his Union Buildings, model for the grander but no more pleasing seat of the Raj government in New Delhi. There are other impressive structures, especially the turn-of-the-century Palace of Justice, described as 'one of the finest classical public spaces in South Africa'. Many of the more impressive edifices front onto Church Square. The Square has always been Pretoria's hub, but nowadays is not a very attractive one. At the time of Union it could have become one of the architectural glories of the sub-continent, embellished with fountains and flowers and Continental-style paving (this was the citizenry's preference). Instead, the civic authorities chose to redesign it as a tramway terminus. Says author Vivien Allen: 'Pretoria exchanged its heart for a public transport system.'

JOHANNESBURG, 60 kilometres south of Pretoria, is the hub of the Witwatersrand conurbation and the country's industrial and financial epicentre. Around and beyond the central area are rings of once-separate dormitory towns, among them Sandton (rich, chic, and in the vanguard of business expansion), Randburg, Roodepoort, Edenvale, Germiston, Alberton, Bedfordview and Soweto, the largest black urban complex in the country. The outer zone includes the substantial centres of Krugersdorp (Dr Jameson's Waterloo, *see* page 35), Randfontein, Westonaria, Kempton Park (which has a fine racetrack), Benoni, Springs and Boksburg. These towns were built on gold, discovered just over a hundred years ago (*see* page 34), which still sustains them but not by any means exclusively – as mentioned, about 40 per cent of the entire country's gross product is generated by the area's huge number of mining, manufacturing, commercial and financial enterprises. Nobody can pretend Johannesburg is a beautiful city. It is notably lacking in open spaces; the mine-dumps are an eyesore (though most of them now have thin coats of greenery; an improvement on the dust-blown past), the crime rate is high. But there is a vibrancy, a bustling, honestly materialistic vitality about the place that does have its appeal. And it has a marvellous climate: it is situated high on the central plateau where the air is rare and heady, the winters clear and not too cold, the summer heat (in good years) relieved by late-afternoon rainstorms that are often cloudbursts of Lear-like proportions.

Johannesburg nightscape. The city is the country's largest.

21

OFTEN IN the telling, perhaps too often, South Africa's story begins with a tiny band of hardy seventeenth-century Dutchmen making their landfall beneath the grandeur of Table Mountain, on the southern tip of the subcontinent, to create the first permanent white settlement on Francis Drake's 'fairest cape'.

That was of course the first significant landmark in the annals of the modern, structured state, but for millennia before southern Africa had been home to darker-skinned people. Archaeological finds indicate that the ancestors of the San, or Bushmen, populated the northern part of the subcontinent as long as 30,000 years ago. They were small bands of nomadic hunter-gatherers who roamed the great sunlit spaces in search of sustenance and solitude, a unique culture that once flourished but has now all but disappeared. For a protracted time, throughout the Later Stone Age, they were the dominant people in the vast area that stretched from today's Namibia eastwards to modern-day KwaZulu-Natal and from the Limpopo to Agulhas on the stormy southern Cape coast.

Not that the word 'dominant', and all that it suggests, is appropriate in the context of San society. Entirely without hostility, these gentle, extraordinary people had – still have – a profound belief in sharing: in co-operation with the family,

Nelson Mandela (*opposite*) walked to freedom in 1990. *Above, from left to right*: In 1938 Afrikaners celebrate the centenary of the Battle of Blood River; Nelson Mandela destroys his pass book, symbol of racial oppression; Soweto's streets erupt in the watershed 1976 student uprising.

between clan and clan, between humans and their environment. Custom and conviction excluded personal antagonism; nature, both animate and inanimate, was sanctified, hallowed in the mystic rituals of the hunt and the trance-like dance, and in the lively cave-paintings and engravings that grace some 2,000 recorded sites throughout southern Africa.

Later on, some of the San clans – the Khoikhoi as they called themselves, which has been roughly translated as 'men of men' – acquired fat-tailed sheep and other livestock from the Sudanese peoples of the north, and in so doing changed the human geography of the region. For the first time the concept of property ownership, and thus of territorial rights, of wealth, status and the imperative to compete, entered into the equation. These new, more acquisitive, more aggressive, semi-nomadic people, who lived and moved (and fought) in well-organized units, were concentrated in three loose groupings – the Korana of the north-central regions of southern Africa, the Einiqua of the west, and the Namaqua of the south-west. Some of the Namaqua moved into what is today Namibia, others filtered down the coast to occupy the rugged plains of Namaqualand, the Cape Peninsula and much of the southern seaboard. It was with these people that the explorers and sea-captains

BY THE TIME THE FIRST **EUROPEANS** PUT DOWN THEIR ROOTS, **BANTU-SPEAKING PEOPLES** WERE WELL ESTABLISHED IN THE REGION

of Portugal, England, France and Holland first came into contact on the shores of the Cape, meetings that usually resulted in mutually profitable barter but occasionally in deadly combat.

At about the same time other, quite different peoples, Negroid-Hamitic pastoralists who (it is thought) originated in the Nilotic north and spoke Bantu languages, had settled in what is now Zimbabwe, and began to migrate across the Limpopo River in about AD 250. A second group, with a more advanced Later Iron Age culture, arrived in the subcontinent some time after 1200. By the time the first Cape Europeans started putting down roots, the Bantu-speakers were well established in many parts of the subcontinent.

Much of the story of black migration is shrouded in mystery, and theories are numerous and complex. It is generally agreed, though, that four main groups were involved: the Sotho, the Nguni, the Tsonga and the Venda. By the late seventeenth century their spearhead, the Xhosa (of the southern Nguni group), were well established in the eastern Cape, on a direct collision course with

the expanding white farming communities. Inevitably, competition for living-space and good grazing would lead to bitter conflict. Inevitably, too, the San population would be depleted almost to the point of extinction through the encroachment of more highly structured, more numerous, more warlike societies – black groups with refined military systems and, because they kept livestock and tilled the soil, an appetite for land.

Some San groups were simply wiped out, or taken captive and absorbed, so introducing their genes into a substantial part of the subcontinent's ethnic composition (and into its culture; the 'click' in some of the languages and many of the animistic beliefs of traditional black societies are of San origin). Others adopted a coastal lifestyle, forsaking the fruits of the veld for those of the sea. Yet others were left alone to pursue their ancient ways because they had made their homes in the immensity of the northern wastelands, the Kalahari regions, in which only they, with their simple needs and special skills, could survive.

Again, much of this can only be guessed at. The story of the south-western clans, though, is a lot less speculative, and profoundly tragic: over the decades, those San who came into contact with the early white settlement at the Cape were hunted to death as 'vermin'. To these people property ownership was an alien, incomprehensible notion: land belonged to all living things, cattle were game, to be taken when hunger so demanded, and their raids into the white settlers' preserve provoked savage retaliation. It appears from the records that up to 200,000 San might have been killed during the first two centuries of colonial occupation.

The other branch of the family, the Khoikhoi, suffered a similar if less genocidal fate, and virtually ceased to exist as a coherent society after white settlement. Many, probably most, succumbed to savage outbreaks of smallpox and other alien epidemics of the eighteenth century. Some of the survivors moved inland to become the half-breed Korana, Griqua, and Oorlam groups. Others remained as 'Colonial Hottentots' (that is, an integral part of the settler-ruled Cape Colony; the word 'Hottentot' was coined by the early Dutch, and is now considered pejorative) and, after the abolition of slavery in the 1830s, mixed with the new freemen, adding their progeny to what eventually became known as the Cape coloured community. Today only a few groups, notably the Nama people of the south-western region of the country and in Namibia, retain an identity clearly traceable to their Khoikhoi origins.

Portuguese navigator, Bartholomeu Dias, acting 'in the service of God our Lord, and to our own advantage', raises a monumental cross on Africa's southern shores in 1488.

THE COMING OF EUROPEANS

In August 1487 two 100-ton caravels and a small store-ship, under the command of Bartholomeu Dias, hoisted full sail in the mouth of the Tagus River and set a south-westerly course into the Atlantic. Sixteen months later Dias was back in Portugal, without any great treasures but with the certain and profoundly valuable knowledge that his ships had rounded the southern tip of Africa. The sea-route to India and the spice-rich Molucca Islands were, at last, open to Portugal's royal fleets.

The curious probability is, though, that his epic voyage was not the first to have taken European explorers around the Cape.

Some two thousand years earlier a flotilla of sturdy Phoenician biremes – double-banked galleys – are thought to have accomplished this feat. Their captains had been charged by Pharaoh Necho to sail down the east coast – that is to say, through the Red Sea and past Zanzibar – and to 'come back through the Pillars of Hercules to the Northern Sea and so to Egypt'. This they duly did and reported, according to the Greek historian Herodotus, 'a thing which I cannot believe, but another man may, namely, in sailing round Libya [the ancient name for Africa], they had the sun on their right hand'. In other words they had coasted westwards past Cape Point.

However that may be, it was the Portuguese of the fifteenth and sixteenth centuries who, 'in the service of God our Lord and to our own advantage', pioneered the modern trade routes. Armed with the most rudimentary of navigational aids – a mariner's compass, instruments to gauge wind direction and an astrolabe to determine latitude – their talented admirals set out to find and chart the sea lane to the treasure-troves of the east. Diego Cão negotiated the arid Namib coast, reaching a point just to the north of present-day Swakopmund in 1486. Two years later Dias ran into the notorious Cape south-easter, allowed his ships to be driven a thousand miles and more into the Atlantic Ocean, then set course first southwards and finally north-east to make his landfall at Mossel Bay – a prodigious exercise in navigational acrobatics that had taken him past the Cape of Storms.

The way was now open, though Dias would enjoy little of the glory – at Algoa Bay, site of modern Port Elizabeth, the votes of his timid travelling companions went against him and he was forced to turn back. It was left to the strong-willed, supremely confident Vasco da Gama, nine years later, to chart a course up the east coast to the busy Islamic outposts of Mozambique (where, to cite the Arab records, his 'ships of the Franks' caused some consternation) and thence across the Indian Ocean to Malabar and beyond.

Thereafter, for over a century, the Iberian commercial empire (Portugal and Spain were united by dynastic marriage in 1580) flourished, providing both a magnet for and a challenge to other, increasingly enterprising, maritime powers. Of these, certainly insofar as the Cape sea lanes to India were concerned, the Dutch were to emerge as the leaders. For much of the sixteenth century the hard-headed merchants of the Netherlands acted as middle-men in the lucrative international spice trade, distributing the precious merchandise throughout a Europe enjoying renascent prosperity, legitimate contributors to business life, welcomed by both supplier and customer.

Less legitimate were the freebooters, who scoured the seas in their swift, well-armed ships in search of the easy pickings provided by galleons heavily laden with the wealth of the Indies and the Americas. But, generally speaking, relations between Antwerp and Lisbon remained amicable enough, until the last decade of the century. Then, for a number of reasons related to the unification of Portugal and Spain, the Dutch decided to go it alone, and to deal directly with the Spice Islands.

Successful reconnaissance expeditions were mounted in the 1590s by the brothers De Houtman and by Jan van Linschoten, whose five-year odyssey produced a rich volume of hitherto secret information on the Portuguese trade and trading regions, all of which he consolidated into his *Itinerario*, published in 1595 and soon to become a kind of mercantile and navigational bible for Holland's seafaring fraternity. Between 1595 and 1602 rival Dutch companies, now competing in earnest for the Moluccan connection, sent a series of fleets to the East Indies, their voyages involving a longer haul across the Indian Ocean than the traditional Portuguese route from Mozambique to Malabar on the Indian subcontinent. The Cape and its watering places therefore became increasingly significant in the calculations of the Dutch navigators.

Both Mossel Bay, which Da Gama had named Angra de São Bras, and Table Bay, known then as Saldanha Bay (the name now belongs to a rocky embayment some 100 kilometres to the north), had been used by Portuguese and other admirals for the previous hundred years as incidental ports of call, natural harbours where there was shelter from storms and where emergency repairs could be effected, fresh water taken from the perennial springs and provisions gained by barter. Indeed, as early as 1501 one devout commander, João da Nova, had erected a small stone church at São Bras, the first European building to be constructed on what is now South African soil.

It was to be half a century, though, before any Dutchman thought of establishing a permanent presence on the southern shore. In due course the competing interests within Holland's mercantile world sank their differences and united under the federal umbrella of the Dutch East India Company, which was formally incorporated, and granted its charter by the States General of the Netherlands in 1602. During the decades that followed, the Company, which had a directorate grandly known as 'The Lords Seventeen', created a maritime empire that elevated tiny Holland to the highest ranks of Europe's nation states. It established a sophisticated administration in the Malayan Archipelago and, after 1619, a permanent far-eastern headquarters at Batavia (Java), the whole supported by a spreading network of garrisoned trading stations called 'comptoirs'.

The Company's decision to create a comptoir at the Cape was more the result of accident than forethought. In 1647 the *Nieuw Haerlem* foundered on the shores of Table Bay and, although the captain and most of the crew were taken on to Holland aboard another vessel – part of a fleet whose passenger list included Jan van Riebeeck – some 60 sailors, under command of junior merchant Leendert Janszen, remained behind at the Cape, sheltered from the elements by a crude fort built of wood salvaged from the wreck. On his return to Holland a full year later Janszen submitted his *Remonstrantie*, a report strongly urging the Company to establish a victualling post at the Cape: a station that would trade peaceably with the local Khoikhoi community, and supply fresh produce to the scurvy-ridden crews of ships bound to and from the East Indies.

On the strength of Janszen's submission, and a carefully argued second opinion by Jan van Riebeeck – the 32-year-old former Company employee who had walked the slopes of Table Mountain a year before and who was now anxious to re-enter Company service – the decision was taken. Scarcely a momentous one in the context of the Dutch East India Company's overall, immense operations – just another small fort manned by a hundred or so men, and this one at the southern end of an unknown land that, according to one jaundiced seafarer, 'yielded nothing to delight the heart of man'. Van Riebeeck was appointed commander and his instructions drawn up. Modestly, and without fanfare, the expedition sailed out of Texel on 24 December 1651.

A stylized view of Cape Town from Table Bay around 1730. By this time the settlers were well established in the immediate hinterland; the first country town, Stellenbosch, had already been founded half a century earlier.

THE FIRST SETTLEMENT

In the practical, prosaic minds of The Lords Seventeen there was no thought of creating a colony at the Cape, let alone a vision of a European Christian state on the African continent. Their agenda was commercial and limited. Nevertheless, a century and a half after Van Riebeeck's landing, when the Dutch finally relinquished control, the makings of such a state were there. The frontiers of white settlement had been pushed 500 kilometres to the east, and 100 kilometres of prosperous farms and vineyards lay to the north and north-east.

At this time – around 1806 – when the British occupied the Cape for the second time – Cape Town was a busy seaport, host to ships of a score of nations and seat of a sophisticated colonial administration. South Africa was a reality – and an uncomfortable one, even then: the clash of cultures, a foretaste of future conflict, was already unfolding; there was antagonism between black and white, between Boer and Briton and, always, the competitive struggle for land. The process had been put in motion, and was irreversible.

However, no such vision of the future visited Jan van Riebeeck, the first commander: he had no aspirations beyond his immediate, functional task. His instructions, which he carried out with stolid Dutch thoroughness, were quite specific: he was to provide for passing Company ships 'the means of procuring herbs, flesh, water and other needful refreshments, and by this means restore the health of the sick'. He was also to build a fort 'in order to take possession of the Cape and so that you cannot be surprised by anyone'. Also among his terms of reference was an order to cultivate the friendship and co-operation of the local inhabitants, and to his credit – and despite his personal opinion that they were a 'savage set, living without conscience' – he did manage to create a mutually profitable and generally amiable relationship with them.

In the 1650s the Peninsula Khoikhoi were divided into three fairly distinct communities. The first to come into contact with the colonists were the Strandlopers ('beach strollers'), more correctly termed the Goringhaicona (which means 'children of the Goringhaqua'), who subsisted on the plants they could gather, on seafood and on the few sheep they kept. Led by 'Harry' (or 'Herry') Autshumao and numbering just a few dozen, they were a disparate folk, bound together by shared poverty and their status as outcasts rather than bonds of kinship.

Larger, more prosperous and generally more sophisticated were the Gorachouqua and the Goringhaiqua, semi-nomadic clans who owned livestock, who lived, albeit in temporary fashion, in reed huts, and who manufactured metal jewellery and cultivated tobacco. It was with these wealthier groups that the settlers bartered copper, iron, brass, alcohol, beads, knives and salt for fresh meat. Farther inland, to the north and west of the Peninsula, were the powerful Cochoqua people.

The Khoikhoi proved hospitable enough, gregarious, eager for trade and quick to adopt alien ways. As early as 1656 the Commander could record that 'they are learning to speak Dutch fairly well ...'. Inevitably, though, territorial encroachment led to sporadic friction: there were raids and counter-raids and two minor, rather inconclusive wars (in 1659 and between 1673 and 1677). Nevertheless, by the end of the century the two races had reached some sort of *modus vivendi*, though the arrangement was hugely biased in favour of the interlopers: the Khoikhoi had been largely dispossessed of their grazing lands, and many were in employment on farms and in town.

COLONIAL ROOTS

Another of the Company's many injunctions to Van Riebeeck, an especially difficult one to accommodate, was the order to establish a self-supporting settlement at the Cape. As the workload increased, so more officials arrived, putting such severe pressure on the white community's modest larder that within two years ships anchored in Table Bay were offloading more supplies than they were taking on.

Van Riebeeck's solution represented a radical change in policy: he turned to private enterprise, releasing a number of men from their Company contracts to set themselves up as independent farmers and traders. Other 'freeburgher' families arrived from Holland. The results were immediate and, for the settler community, gratifying: in its very first, experimental year – 1656 – the block of land set aside at Rondebosch produced a bumper crop of wheat, enough for local needs and some to spare. A small beginning, perhaps, but a profoundly significant one: the Cape was now no longer a commercial garrison with strictly limited objectives but a permanent colony capable of growth. The move marked the start of the settlement proper.

Over the years the freeburghers grew in number, steadily pushing out the frontiers of European settlement – to the Hottentots Holland region in the 1670s and to Stellenbosch nine years later. This charming little centre was named after Simon van der Stel, the innovative governor of the Cape from 1679 to century's end. He had earmarked the district as an ideal wheat-producing area, and the farms established there paid such handsome dividends that very soon there was an over-supply and the emphasis was shifted to the growing of grapes and the making of wine.

Not that this was a new idea. Van Riebeeck himself took a deep interest in viticulture and, a mere month after setting foot ashore in 1652, had placed an order with Amsterdam for seeds and plants 'and also vines, which ought to thrive as well on local hill slopes as they do in Spain and France'. He received his stock and by 2 February 1659 was able to confide to his journal that 'Today, praise be to God, wine can be made for the first time from Cape grapes ...'. The first vineyard, on his farm Boschheuval (now the Cape Town suburb of Bishopscourt), contained just 12,000 vines; 30 years later the vineyards had spread their gracious mantle over much of the hinterland. By 1750 there were 4 million vines growing around the pretty little country towns of Stellenbosch, Paarl and Franschhoek.

Immigrants continued to trickle in from Europe. Most were Dutch, though there was a sprinkling of Flemings, Scandinavians and, especially, Germans. By the time the whites of the Cape had grown to a thousand in number, in 1688, they were joined by a group of particularly welcome newcomers – the sober and industrious Huguenots. These were French Protestants who, after the Edict of Nantes was revoked to expose them to religious persecution, fled to pastures new and far.

The first Cape European houses were modest, single-storeyed, flat-roofed affairs of sun-dried brick, the white-washed walls and green-painted woodwork lending a certain charm to the town. In the country areas the settlers built more substantial homes, often of stone, reed-thatched, thick-walled (for defence) and functional. With prosperity, though, a distinctive style began to evolve: gabled, half-shuttered buildings, the entrance-ways an impressive focal point through which one walked into a spacious *voorhuis*. These farmsteads were constructed symmetrically, even severely, to 'T', 'H' and 'U' shapes. As the decades passed, the cold lines of the grander ones were softened with the addition of wings, courtyards that encircled the stables, slave quarters and other outbuildings. Thus emerged the renowned Cape Dutch architectural style, some lovely examples of which still grace the Peninsula and its northern and eastern hinterland. The style represented, in part, an attempt by the Dutch settlers to re-create something of their beloved homeland but, curiously enough, many of the early architectural elements were derived not from Holland but from the East, and were introduced by 'Malay' slaves skilled in the building crafts.

MASTERS AND SERVANTS

Slavery was a prominent feature of Cape community life for almost two centuries. The early colonists were inhibitively short of labour, both skilled and unskilled; Van Riebeeck was unable to recruit the local Khoikhoi in numbers, and a formal decision to import slaves was taken. In retrospect the move, indeed the entire system, was iniquitous, but it was by no means exclusive to the Cape: slave trading and owning was common practice in much of the world until the 1830s; across the Atlantic a brutal civil war was fought over the issue in the 1860s.

The first slave to arrive was a stowaway from Batavia (Java) who arrived in the March of 1653, but the inflow really began five years later when the *Amersfoort* acquired 500 slaves from a Portuguese ship and offloaded them in Table Bay. Thereafter, demand from the wheat- and wine-farmers ensured a steady growth in numbers, despite the cost (up to 100 gulden a head) and high incidence of runaways, some of whom joined the mixed Oorlam and Griqua communities of the distant Orange River (now known as the Gariep River) region. By 1710 there were about 1,200 adult slaves at the Cape; in 1795, when the British took over, the figure had risen to 17,000 – a number somewhat larger than that of the white population. They were brought, originally, from places as far afield as Guinea and Angola on Africa's west coast, Delagoa Bay (now Maputo) on the east coast, from Madagascar, Ceylon (Sri Lanka), Batavia (Indonesia) and Malaya (Malaysia). After the initial influx, importation dwindled to a trickle: children born to slave parents accounted for the steady rate of increase. The few who were released from bondage were known as 'free blacks'.

It was during this initial phase of modern South African history – the century and a half after the first landing – that the pattern of race prejudice and race dominance was established. Whites owned most of the land in the occupied areas and they were in authority at every level of administration and of the economy. The status of other peoples – Khoikhoi, slaves and, later, blacks of the Xhosa region to the east – was restricted for the most part to that of labourer. The great majority of people of colour of that period were unskilled and would remain so by settler law because, in practical terms, there was no real need for an infusion of expertise during the pre-industrial era. Nor was there any incentive to encourage the growth of a non-white middle class in a region that was, after all, largely a rural backwater.

Under Dutch rule, segregation became entrenched. Social mixing, which was fairly common in the infant colony, became rare, and those who married across the colour line were cold-shouldered by the establishment. There was increasing discrimination, too, within the only recognized religious institution, the Dutch Reformed Church, which began to keep race-based records and, from about the 1820s, to hold separate services for colour-defined congregations. The rights of slaves were, by definition, severely restricted until emancipation in the 1830s. Those of technically free people of colour came under sustained official assault from the 1780s, when the government began to operate a system of indentured (and in some cases forced) labour and introduced 'passes' that limited freedom of movement.

Probably the most important development of all during this period, though, was one of attitude. Decades of reliance on slavery and a cheap, mostly submissive labour force created a kind of master-race mentality, a conviction among whites that they were innately superior and that somehow this had been preordained. The psychology, inherited by succeeding generations, eventually lent moral force to the evolution of the most immoral of societies.

THE ROAD TO THE EAST

Like any frontier community, the early Cape settlers had their share of enterprising explorers. Forays into the northern interior were launched by Wintervogel (who reached present-day Malmesbury); Gabbema (the Berg River Valley and Paarl, which he named after the giant granite boulders that dominate the area – depending on the light they often gleam like pearls); Danckaert (the Cedarberg and Olifants River, named for a herd of 300 elephant he saw); and Van Meerhoff (Namaqualand). Van der Stel himself led an expedition to the copper mountains of Namaqualand in 1685. A hundred years after Van Riebeeck's

landing Jacobus Coetsee, a captain of the burgher dragoons, crossed the Orange River and wandered over the high plateau for some months. The eastern horizons were broadened by, among others, Hieronimus Cruse in the late 1660s: he trekked overland to Mossel Bay and heard tell of 'darker-skinned men' – that is to say, the Xhosa, who were by then long settled in the east and were advancing along the southern coastal belt. Shortly afterwards the settlers got to know more about these mysterious black people with the stranding, in 1686, of the Dutch ship *Stavenisse* some distance south of the future Port Natal: the rescue parties produced eye-witness accounts of the Xhosa around the Kei River.

Settlement of the eastern districts received its first major impetus when, in 1699, Governor Willem Adriaan van der Stel (Simon's second son) reversed Company policy, which had hitherto discouraged stock-farmers from trekking. Throughout the eighteenth century the frontiers were pushed steadily outwards to the north and east by the relentless advance of trekboers – nomadic farmers moving ever farther out, in quest of grazing and away from the restrictions of formal government. New magisterial districts, each controlled by an official known as a landdrost, were established as the land was tamed and homesteads built.

In 1745 a new drostdy – as the regional headquarters of the magistrate or landdrost were called – was established in the attractive little village which, two years later, was to be named Swellendam. By mid-century the boundary of the Cape of Good Hope had reached the Great Brak River near Mossel Bay and farms were appearing as far away as the west bank of the Gamtoos. By the 1780s settlers had moved farther eastwards and were putting down their roots along the Great Fish River, and before the decade was out the town and district of Graaff-Reinet had been formally proclaimed. By this time the central administration in Cape Town was at acrimonious odds with the farther reaches of its eastern domains. Ruggedly individualistic frontiersmen, resenting distant and what they regarded as misguided control over their economic life, and the Company's handling of the Xhosa problem, declared (briefly) their own independent republics: Graaff-Reinet in February 1795 and Swellendam four months later.

In fact the physical power of the Dutch East India Company, and therefore the strength of its administrative muscle in the region, had been declining since the early 1700s. Towards the end of the century, after four debilitating Anglo-Dutch wars, France and England had emerged as the leading European protagonists, rivals in the quest for, among other things, control of the oceans. The Cape, weakly garrisoned and strategically positioned on the sea-routes, was a tempting prize. British troops landed at Muizenberg in July 1795, though six weeks were to pass before the local militia, of which coloured troops formed a substantial component, could be defeated at Wynberg Hill.

The Dutch capitulation, signed at Rondebosch on the 16 September, inaugurated a period of direct rule from Whitehall that, with one brief break (the interregnum of 1802–1803, when the Dutch, in the persons of the admirable Jacob de Mist and Jan Janssens, returned to govern the Cape), was to underpin events on the subcontinent for the next hundred years and more – until the Act of Union of 1910 created the all-but-sovereign state of South Africa.

The early Heerengracht, Cape Town's main thoroughfare. At its southern end lay the graceful Company's Gardens, a place of oak-shaded avenues and exotic plants.

THE BRITISH PRESENCE

The country that the British soldiers took over was still very much a backwater in the flow of international affairs. True, Cape Town had grown, but at the end of the eighteenth century it still comprised little more than a cluster of 2,000 or so houses that sprawled from the jettied dockside up and around the lower slopes of Table Mountain. Along the Liesbeek River there were a few still-rural villages that were later to become the swathe of suburbia stretching from Woodstock to Wynberg; farther afield lay a hinterland of prosperous wheat and wine farms, and the remote and troubled eastern border area.

The town itself was attractive enough, its pride the Gardens, started by the first settlers as a humble vegetable patch but now assuming a more decorative rôle. Indeed as early as 1685 the visiting scholar Abbé de Choisy could observe that he 'would have liked to see it in a corner of Versailles'. Oaks and ashes shaded its more mundane plants; a pleasure lodge had been added in 1700 (later, some think, rebuilt to become Government House, now known as the Tuynhuys). Leading from harbour to garden was the elegant, stone-paved, oak-lined Heerengracht – present-day Adderley Street. Other features contributed substance and, if not sophistication, certainly charm to the place: the leisurely spaciousness of the Grand Parade; some beautiful private residences, the Cape style perhaps best exemplified by the pleasantly solid Koopmans de Wet House on Strand Street; the massive Castle on what was then the waterfront, and of course the town's busy, warren-like dockland. Cape Town had become one of the foremost ports of the southern hemisphere, host to ships and sailors of a dozen nations and already famed as the 'tavern of the seas', its clubs and pubs proliferating, its streets alive with horse-drawn traffic and the press of polyglot humanity.

Indeed, as colonial headquarters went, the new British administrators could have been a great deal worse off. They settled themselves in comfortably after the second occupation, in 1806, and addressed the issues of government: slavery; the growing spirit of independence among the Boers of the outlying regions; the angry Xhosa on the eastern border, and the need to economize (Britain had incurred a huge war debt during the Napoleonic struggles).

In 1806 the colony's population comprised 26,000 whites, some 30,000 slaves, 20,000 Khoikhoi and uncountable numbers of San and Bantu-speaking people beyond the Great Fish River, resentful of and posing a constant threat to the invasive border settlements.

The first full-scale 'frontier war' had erupted in 1779; altogether, there would be eight more over the next hundred years, during which time the border would be moved progressively eastwards to the Kei River. Of this series of skirmishes, probably the most significant was the fifth, in 1819, when the Xhosa army mounted a direct attack on Grahamstown. This was repulsed by the garrison but the event persuaded Governor Lord Charles Somerset that only massive immigration could bring any semblance of stability to the troubled areas. Conviction was translated into action with the landing in Algoa Bay, in 1820, of 60 parties of English, Scots and Irish families numbering some 4,000 men, women and children: a small fraction of the 90,000 who had applied to emigrate but enough, the authorities decided, to populate and 'pacify' the recently proclaimed Albany district of the eastern Cape – the vast area covering most of the disputed territory between the Bushmans and Great Fish rivers and from Grahamstown to the coast.

The settlers suffered five years of bitter hardship and disappointment on the unforgiving land: conditions were primitive; equipment rudimentary; the allotments too small; the ban on recruiting labour from among the Xhosa clans a prohibitive restriction; the depredations of drought, locust and Xhosa unrelenting. Few survived as farmers, most of them drifting into the villages and small towns, originally military garrisons, that now studded the eastern Cape countryside. Nevertheless, the pioneer scheme was not a total failure in the context of the British colonial administration's priorities, high among which was the creation of a white-inhabited 'buffer' region in the east. Four thousand new settlers might not seem a very substantial number by modern standards, but it increased the colony's white population by a full 10 per cent.

Towards the end of the 1830s, too, an organized community of Britons put its first, tentative roots down on the far eastern coast. Since 1824 there had been a small trading post at Port Natal, and white hunters stalked the thickly wooded hinterland in search of elephant and ivory. They were tolerated, even welcomed, by the powerful Zulu king Shaka. They were transients rather than colonists, even if they did hold land – 9,000 square kilometres around the bay – under a royal, though vague, grant. In time the place was renamed Durban, and during the course of the nineteenth century, large-scale immigration schemes ensured both its growth and Natal's quintessentially English character. But for the first decade or so the settlement remained small and vulnerable, its affairs intimately bound up with the eastern prong of the Great Trek.

A trekboer wagon. These early migrants – semi-nomadic herders for the most part – had wandered the great spaces of the interior for generations before the Great Trek of the 1830s.

THE OUTWARD URGE

In the mid-1830s there began an exodus of Boers from the volatile eastern Cape. Families gathered in parties, inspanned their oxen and headed into the immense and little-known (but by no means depopulated; its 'emptiness' was a myth later used to justify conquest) northern and north-eastern interior. The migration, apparently spontaneous in its initial thrust but in fact well organized, started in a modest way, gathered momentum over the next few turbulent years and eventually, when the sound of battle had died away and the wanderers became farmers again, succeeded in doubling the area of white settlement in Africa.

Arguments about the nature of the Great Trek are numerous and conflicting. To the dispassionate historian it was just one more movement of peoples in search of Lebensraum in a century characterized by mass-migrations, comparable perhaps to the westward advance of the American pioneers. To the Afrikaners it remains a heroic saga, fount of their republican traditions and of their national identity. To British officialdom of the time and later it was a catastrophe, the origin of a divided country, the trigger for deep and lasting dissension between Boer, Briton and black people. To blacks the Trek appeared simply as a blatant land-grab. What is not in dispute is that, in the end, the Afrikaner nation did manage to occupy huge territories between the Orange and the Limpopo, to establish independent republics and, ultimately, to wage a long and bitter war against the British Empire. It was, without doubt, the most crucial event in the story of pre-democratic South Africa.

Much has been said of the Trek's causes: of the ruinous losses suffered by Boer homesteaders in the exposed eastern frontier region; of shortage of capital, the devaluation of the local rixdollar against sterling and the massive accumulation of debt; of the lack of military support from the British authorities in Cape Town; of the colonial government's 'over-reactive' respect for the status and rights of black people, inspired by philanthropists in London and Scottish missionaries on the ground; of the abolition of slavery and the consequent rise in labour costs; and above all of British meddling in and control over the affairs of independent-minded frontiersmen (whose resentment of interference, in fact, stretched back to the days of the Dutch East India Company). The essence of the whole matter was more simply, if rather ruggedly, explained to an English resident of Bathurst in the 1830s. The Boer said that 'in his father's lifetime and his own they had been five times clean swept out by [Xhosa raiders] ... but in those old times when they were robbed they redressed the matter themselves, but now their hands were tied while [the Xhosa's] were loose'.

There was, though, a more positive side to the Great Trek: the Boer people were not simply running away from an intolerable situation; they were moving towards what they perceived as their Promised Land. They knew a little of what lay in the vast interior beyond; earlier migrants had preceded them, individual trekboers who had wandered the northern veld for generations in search of better grazing and hunting grounds. From the information that filtered back the prospects of finding peace and solitude appeared bright enough to merit exploration, if for no other reason than that many of the eastern and northern regions had been subjected to the ravages of what is known as the *Mfecane*, or *Difaqane* (the Sotho term), a cataclysm that had apparently reduced the size of many of the indigenous populations and distorted and weakened traditional inter-tribal affiliations, both of which, for different reasons, encouraged intrusive settlement.

WARRIOR SUPREME

To digress a little from the Great Trek (though the two events were closely interactive), the *Mfecane*, in its simplest definition, was the forced migration of millions of black people, initially to the west and north of Zululand and eventually over most of the northern subcontinent. It began when Shaka, leader of the Zulus and warrior supreme, cleared his immediate neighbourhood of all opposition and set out on the bloody road of conquest, helping to ignite a massive chain reaction of violence and counter-violence. Other disruptive forces were also at work, notably drought, competition for land and water, the slave raiders of the Mozambique seaboard and the colonial British of the eastern Cape, whose advance into Xhosa country led to dispossession, and migration, on a significant scale. Defeated groups would move on, displacing others, who in turn migrated to spread fire, sword and famine in farther reaches. It was the domino principle in classic and devastating action.

Shaka was born in 1788, the son of Senzsangakona, chief of the small Zulu clan – to which his mother Nandi also belonged,

A colonial artist's impression of Shaka. Within the space of just two years the great warrior-king transformed one of the smaller, weaker Nguni clans into the most powerful of African nations.

the marriage thus breaking customary law. She and the six-year-old boy were forced out of their natal community, taking refuge with the neighbouring Llangeni people. But mother and son remained under a stigma, and in 1802 they were again expelled. They found new protection with Dingiswayo and his powerful Mthethwa group.

In due course Shaka served his adoptive people as an outstanding military commander before succeeding to the Zulu chieftainship in 1816 – initially not the most promising of offices since the Zulu were a very small part of the broader Nguni cultural and linguistic grouping (the clan numbered a bare 1,500). Nevertheless his genius, and the ruthless discipline he imposed, immediately transformed the character, and the power, of the Zulu.

His first priority was the reorganization of his small army, its weapons and battle tactics. He replaced the ineffectual throwing spear with the long-bladed stabbing assegai, forcing his soldiers into close combat. He also refined the age-graded regimental system (the *amabutho*) which other Nguni groups to the north had introduced with success: soldiers now lived with men their own age, in their own quarters, and each regiment had its own markings and regalia – all in all, a transformation that endowed his army with formidable *esprit de corps*. Finally, Shaka developed

the famed Zulu fighting machine. The regiments in the field, collectively known as the impi, were split into four divisions, deployed roughly in the shape of an ox. The most powerful section (the 'chest') clashed head-on with the enemy while the second and third (the 'horns') flanked and encircled. The fourth remained a mobile reserve. And Shaka fought not just to win but to exterminate – a new approach to warfare which, until then, had often amounted to virtually bloodless encounters, the weaker force retiring quickly from the field after a token exchange of throwing spears.

The story of the *Mfecane* is prohibitively complex, but mention of two or three of the migrations may convey just how radically it changed the human landscape of southern Africa.

Shaka launched his first attack on Matiwane's powerful Ngwane clan in the eastern foothills of the Drakensberg. Matiwane moved on, southwards and westwards, to assault the southern Nguni and the Sotho of the uplands, who scattered to cause havoc elsewhere.

Under the inspired leadership of Moshoeshoe, refugees from the *Mfecane* joined Sotho-speakers and others, and retreated into the fastness of the highlands of today's Lesotho to found a new kingdom.

Mzilikazi, perhaps Shaka's most enterprising general, quarrelled with his king and fled north with a 'raiding kingdom' that grew as he conquered and absorbed tribe after tribe. His destructive path led him to the Olifants River and then westwards into Sotho territory. Eventually he was defeated in what was to become the Transvaal by a mixed force of trekkers, Griqua and Tswana, and moved on, across the Limpopo River, to establish the Matabele empire.

Two other groups were founded by disaffected Zulu commanders: Soshangane, who led his impis into Mozambique (the Shangaans); and Zwangendaba, who settled 2,000 kilometres to the north, around Lake Malawi (the Angoni).

TREKKING ON

Meanwhile, the Boers migrated, first in their hundreds and then in their thousands. Some saw Natal as their ultimate haven and crossed the eastern reaches of the Orange (Gariep) River. By the middle of 1837 they had gathered at a place between Thaba Nchu and the Vet River from where an advance party, led by Piet Retief, set off eastwards towards Durban and beyond, into Zululand. Shaka's successor, Dingane, received Retief with deceptive amiability and by December the main body of trekkers, encouraged by the promise of land south of the Tugela River, had hauled their wagons over the high Drakensberg. After concluding the formal treaty, however, Retief and his party of 69 were killed, and Dingane's impis went on to attack the trekker camps in a series of fierce engagements at Bloukrans, Bushman's River and elsewhere. The Boers suffered grievous casualties but by the end of 1838 they had managed to rally their forces. On 16 December, after a night spent in prayer and in the offering up of the formal vow, or covenant, at a place later known to white South Africans as Blood River, their muskets and laagered discipline routed the Zulu army.

The Boer Republic of Natalia was destined to be short-lived. In May 1842 British troops occupying Durban were besieged by the Boers, but succeeded in summoning reinforcements (this was the occasion of Dick King's renowned 1,500-kilometre ride to enlist the help of the garrison of Grahamstown) and the four-year-old state disintegrated. Some of the Boers returned to the Cape; most rejoined the main body of northern Voortrekkers.

These had in the meantime been busy preparing the way for settlement of the land beyond the Orange River. During the next decade numerous small groups took their wagon-trains over enormous tracts of inhospitable country. Andries Potgieter's party pushed the farthest north, crossing the Limpopo into present-day Zimbabwe as early as 1836. Van Rensburg's was annihilated in Mozambique. Louis Trichardt's odyssey took him first to the northern Transvaal's Soutpansberg and then south-east through fever-ridden Mozambique to Delagoa Bay (modern Maputo). Here both he and his wife died and the remnants of his decimated group took a ship to Durban.

By the mid-1850s, however, the Boers had settled in sufficient numbers to warrant the establishment and formal recognition of two viable independent states, one between the Orange and the Vaal rivers, the other to the north of this, between the Vaal and the Limpopo.

TWO REPUBLICS, TWO COLONIES

From about the middle of the nineteenth century onwards southern Africa comprised four major and a number of less substantial white political entities. They interacted, of course, but for the most part functioned separately, and continued to do so until Union in 1910. The web of events is intricate. In broad outline, however:
• The country that was to become the Orange Free State – that is to say, the land between the Orange and the Vaal rivers – had been

Paul Kruger, long-serving president of the Boer republic of the Transvaal and regarded as the 'Father of Afrikanerdom'. He died, a bitter man, in 1904.

infiltrated by a few trekboers during the early pioneering years, but it was only with the northward advance of the Voortrekkers from 1835 that white settlement began in earnest. The small town of Winburg (named not for some grand victory but following the resolution of a local argument) was founded in 1837 as the 'capital' of the new territory. This decision turned out to be somewhat premature since the trekkers were still too divided to form a coherent state. Their lack of unity, and a confusing element of black-white confrontation over land rights and frontiers, prompted the British to annex the area and to create the Orange River Sovereignty in 1848. Bloemfontein, then scarcely more than a schoolroom and a cluster of white-washed cottages, was declared the administrative centre and headquarters of the British Resident.

None of these events succeeded in bringing stability to the region: at one point the Boers rose in revolt, and were defeated at the battle of Boomplaats by a force commanded by the Cape colonial governor Sir Harry Smith. Finally, though, following the Bloemfontein Convention in 1854, Britain recognized the independence of the new Republic of the Orange Free State. Real progress was achieved under the steady guidance of Jan Brand, president for the 24 crucial and crisis-ridden years between 1864 and 1888. Brand accepted British dominance on the subcontinent but stoically resisted moves, principally by Lord Carnarvon, the colonial secretary, to bring about a confederation of southern African states. However, the discovery of diamond-fields in the northern Cape in 1867 brought prosperity and political muscle, both of which were reinforced with the arrival of the railway in 1888 and the customs agreement with the Cape a year later.
• The Transvaal's constitutional course was similar, though from the very beginning its settlers tended to be less tractable, more hostile to British influence than those of the Orange Free State. Many of the Boer intransigents, for instance, crossed the Vaal into the northern bastion after the battle of Boomplaats in 1848.

Independence was conferred on the Transvaal, or more correctly the South African Republic, at the Sand River Convention of 1852. Four years later, despite religious controversy and a great deal of quarrelsome rivalry among the local leaders (much of the territory had been carved up into mini-republics), the country finally managed to elect its first president, Marthinus Pretorius, and adopt a formal constitution.

During the confederation issue of the late 1870s the Transvaal, predictably, proved the most isolationist of the four white communities, a fact which almost certainly contributed to its formal annexation by British troops under the Natal secretary for native affairs, Sir Theophilus Shepstone, in 1877 (the official reason given for the occupation was fear of open conflict between Zulu and Transvaler – a reason which became invalid after the Zulu empire was finally crushed at Ulundi in 1879). On 16 December 1880 the Boer leaders, who now included one Paul Kruger, reproclaimed their republic, and went to war. Three months later, on the bloody slopes of Majuba Hill, their forces inflicted the first and only major defeat suffered by Britain during the whole of Queen Victoria's long reign. Shortly afterwards, at the Convention of Pretoria, the right to internal self-government was restored to the South African Republic.

Majuba marked one more step on the road to the collapse of Boer-Briton accommodation in southern Africa. For the British, it meant humiliation, and a determination in the corridors of Imperial power to salvage national prestige and pride. For the Boers, it was positive affirmation of their strength as a united people and of their ability to preserve their national independence come what may.

• The Cape, meanwhile, had been progressing as steadily if more sedately towards constitutional maturity. By the end of the century the eastern and north-eastern borders had stabilized, the former with the establishment of the port of East London and the development of small inland settlements, most starting life as garrisons. The frontiers were finally and formally fixed with the annexation of Pondoland adjoining Natal and, in 1895, of British Bechuanaland (approximately modern Botswana), a huge northern wilderness area sprawling between the Transvaal and the Namibia of today. The mountain fortress of Basutoland, which was eventually to become the kingdom of Lesotho, had fallen under the Cape administration in 1871 before reverting to direct British control in 1884.

For nearly 30 years after the second British occupation the Cape Colony had been ruled, autocratically, by a Whitehall-appointed governor. In 1834, however, a small concession was made to the democratic process with the appearance of a nominated legislative council which included five white colonials. Twenty years later, in 1854, came representative government: a parliament containing a majority of elected members, but without executive control, which still resided in the office of governor. This final authority was granted the colonists with the establishment in 1872 of responsible government modelled on the Westminster system, and the institution of a fully elected parliament with virtually complete powers to conduct the colony's internal affairs. The Imperial voice was henceforth to be heard, chiefly in matters of foreign policy, through an appointed high commissioner. Qualifications for the franchise were on the basis of income and property rather than colour.

• The second of nineteenth-century southern Africa's self-governing colonies, Natal, had been annexed to the Cape after the demise of the Boer republic of Natalia in 1844, but became a separate entity, administered by a lieutenant-governor, the following year. Large-scale private immigration schemes towards the end of the decade stimulated rapid growth during the second half of the century. In 1856 there were about 8,000 white settlers in Durban and its lush hinterland, which still teemed with wild game (elephants were foraging close to the city well into the twentieth century). By 1893 the figure had risen to 50,000, with Durban shortly to become one of the biggest and busiest ports south of the equator.

Throughout the century, though, and to the present day, the Zulu population of the region was in the overwhelming majority. There were efforts to safeguard 'native' land rights, but cynical politics intruded during the 1870s: Cetshwayo's powerful (but patently peaceful) Zulu nation was considered a threat to Britain's 'confederal' schemes, which envisaged a loosely unified southern Africa firmly within the Imperial sphere of influence, and in January 1879, on the flimsiest of pretexts, British troops under Lord Chelmsford marched into Zululand in a deliberate and unprovoked attempt to conquer a neutral territory. The attempt almost failed: a 1,300-strong invading force was annihilated at Isandlwana, but the heroic and

well-publicized sideshow at Rorke's Drift restored some British pride, and in due course the lightly armed, remarkably brave Zulu regiments were cut to pieces, by superior firepower, at Khambula and, finally, with the loss of 10,000 lives, at Ulundi. Zululand was then ruthlessly balkanized, divided into 13 separate chieftaincies and, in 1887, annexed to Britain before being incorporated into the Colony of Natal four years later.

The last ingredient of southern Africa's heterogeneous society was added to the ethnic stew in the years after the arrival of the first indentured labourers from India in 1860 (see page 14). They were followed to Natal's newly established sugar plantations by a steady stream of Asian migrants. By the turn of the century they, too, outnumbered the colony's white inhabitants.

Thus by the latter half of the 1800s the subcontinent's kaleidoscopic make-up – a mix of peoples of distinct and different identities bound together by history and by geography but of differing cultures and, perhaps inevitably, of conflicting interests – had been established: Briton, Afrikaner and coloured in the western Cape; Xhosa and white in the eastern Cape; Zulu, Asian and Briton in Natal; Boer and black in the two republics, with a horde of *uitlanders* – foreigners – poised to invade the about-to-be-discovered goldfields on the Witwatersrand in the Transvaal.

RACE AND RIFT
Some of the stronger foundations of the segregated society were laid in the decade following the Great Trek. Among the reasons the Boers left the Cape and its troubled frontier regions in such numbers was their resentment of official British colonial policy, which placed emphasis on race equality and, at times, on assimilation. For these tough, Calvinistic people, compromise was unthinkable: there was to be no parity, no equitable sharing of resources and opportunities and, most certainly, no integration. The land within the borders of their republics was theirs by right of conquest, and the task they set themselves was simple and exclusive: to survive, and to preserve their religion and new-found national identity against all threats. Foremost among the latter, by their reckoning, were the meddlesome British officials they had left behind and, all around them, the great and potentially overwhelming mass of black Africans.

The first Transvaal constitution bluntly stated the case. The burghers, it said, 'desire to permit no equality of status between Coloured people and the white inhabitants, either in Church or State'. Nor was there to be any form of partnership, or 'trusteeship', unless it be between master and servant. The concept of dignified co-existence, or of defined and protected territories set aside for blacks and within which traditional cultures would be allowed to develop, was not part of the republican Boer's philosophy. Only much later, when blacks began entering the urban economies in large numbers, did Afrikanerdom embrace such ideas.

Trusteeship, though, did feature in British Cape frontier policy. Some influential people – most notably the administrator Andries Stockenström – strongly urged his superiors in London to halt the processes of conquest and expansion, to define the borders between the black and white territories, to leave the Xhosa alone to live their own lives, and to formalize black-white relations through a series of treaties. Stockenström's 'treaty system' was at base a form of what was later to become apartheid of the grander kind (as opposed to 'petty apartheid'), but in the nature of the times it was progressive, and for a while it seemed it might even succeed. In due course, however, the frontier farmers resumed their eastward encroachment, the impetus fuelled by plain greed on the one hand and by British enthusiasm for 'civilizing', and therefore controlling, on the other. And finally the frontier policy was reversed yet again with the passage of the 1894 Glen Grey Act, which introduced individual land tenure and a mild form of self-government to the Xhosa territories of the Transkei. The Glen Grey Act has been regarded as the first important move to allow black people their basic rights. But it also represented a major, indeed crucial, change in British thinking – from optimistic faith that the two races could live together in harmony, to a conviction that they could not

The pattern was similar in nineteenth-century Natal, where Native Affairs secretary Sir Theophilus Shepstone contrived his own version of territorial apartheid. This, when one comes down to it, amounted to little more than confining and controlling the movement of black people by means of a pass system. In neither the Cape nor Natal, in fact, was British liberalism seen at its best. Perhaps the problems ran too deep for a dispassionately benevolent authority, thousands of miles away in London's Whitehall, to solve by proxy.

The race equation in the Cape was rather more complex than elsewhere. Ordinance No. 50 of 1828 did confer full rights and equality before the law on the Cape coloured community, but race and class distinctions continued to prove powerful barriers to free social and political intercourse. Moreover, a series of harsh 'masters and servants' statutes kept the majority of Cape workers in effective subjection. And, although the Cape constitution of 1854 was technically colour-blind, the voting qualifications were so high that they excluded all but a few people of colour.

DIAMONDS, GOLD AND WAR

The discovery, in 1867, of the fabulous diamond-fields of Griqualand West, north of the Cape Colony, was a watershed event: it marked the metamorphosis of what had until then been regarded by Britain as a strategic backwater, in some respects more a troublesome nuisance than an Imperial asset, into a very valuable colonial possession.

Prospectors, diggers, drifters, chancers and a fair sprinkling of honest men converged on the fields from all parts of the globe, though there was a preponderance of Cape Britons among the men who were to demolish the original diamond hill, create Kimberley's Big Hole and exploit the world's richest source of the shiny precious stones.

Problems there were aplenty during the first few frenetic years of the diamond rush: fortunes were made (and lost) overnight; men lit their cigars with 10 pound notes, and the champagne flowed, but there was a seamier side to life in the dusty, unkempt settlement of tents, shacks and the odd brick building. Within a very short time the population of Kimberley exceeded that of Cape Town, but its residents enjoyed practically none of the amenities, civic or social, of the older city. Crime was rife, alcohol and gambling the major preoccupations, and political unrest a sporadic and rowdy feature of the early years. Britain annexed Griqualand West in 1871, ruled directly for nine years and then, in 1880, incorporated the territory into the Cape Colony. By this time Kimberley had settled down into a more humdrum routine, its respectable air of permanence derived largely from the stability brought to the fields by a young financial genius named Cecil John Rhodes.

Rhodes had emigrated from England as a sickly 17-year-old and made his way without too much delay to the boom town. Within

Kimberley's De Beers mine, later to be known as the Big Hole, in 1872. By the end of its life it had yielded up more than three tons of top-grade diamonds.

10 years he had consolidated the small-claim workings under his giant De Beers umbrella (and later bought out the flamboyant Barney Barnato's almost-as-substantial holdings) and, by the mid-1880s, was in control of the international diamond trade. This provided the platform from which he would launch his meteoric career as a politician and empire-builder. Already his vision, which encompassed no less than an Africa painted Imperial red from Cape to Cairo, had taken shape in his mind.

Of greater political significance was the accidental discovery, in July 1886, of gold in the Transvaal – the world's biggest field – on the Witwatersrand, just 50 kilometres from the Boer capital Pretoria. Paul Kruger, now president of the South African Republic, viewed the rapid influx of *uitlanders* (foreigners) with a wary eye. His strained treasury desperately needed the revenue from the mines and from the 'concessions' – monopolies – he liberally granted to suppliers of everything from beer to dynamite, but the new-comers threatened to overwhelm his small and jealously

In ambush mode. By the end of 1900, the battles and sieges of the Anglo-Boer War had given way to an exhausting, devastating game of hide-and-seek that was played across the vast spaces of the interior of what was to become South Africa; Boer guerrillas such as these repeatedly hit at British outposts and the region's vital lines of communication.

newly acquired territory across the Limpopo (known as Rhodesia) began their famed but ill-judged ride from the Bechuanaland border towards Pretoria and Johannesburg.

The Jameson Raid was the product of a consipracy which had four major elements: Cecil Rhodes, now prime minister of the Cape Colony and determined to bring the gold-rich Transvaal into the Imperial fold; the Reform Committee, representing the *uitlanders*; Dr Jameson, Rhodes's man in the field, an adventurous soul who saw himself as Clive of India reincarnate; and finally the powerful British colonial secretary, Joseph Chamberlain, whose complicity was covert but real enough. Of all these, only the bumbling Reform Committee was inspired by a genuine desire to rectify wrongs; the main aim of the others was straight-forward territorial conquest.

The plan, which called for precise synchronization between the Raid and a popular uprising in Johannesburg, misfired badly. Jameson and his men were defeated, captured, tried and convicted, but, in a masterstroke of public relations, Kruger saw to it that conspirators served only brief jail sentences.

THE ANGLO-BOER WAR

Anglo-Boer relations plummeted to a new low. All Kruger's suspicions of Britain's perfidy and her designs on his republic and its gold seemed to be confirmed. Indeed they were entirely justified during the next two years. Chamberlain and his representative at the Cape, the arch-Imperialist Alfred Milner, were more set than ever on the 'unification of Southern Africa' – a euphemism for bringing the Transvaal within the British sphere, by negotiation if possible, by force if necessary. In the long, weary months of diplomatic exchange and conference the Boer leadership tried desperately to avoid the final breach, conceding to Milner's demands for *uitlander* rights only to find, again and again, that there were other, harsher, demands to follow. Eventually the high commissioner insisted that 'There is no way out except reform in the Transvaal or war'. Replied Kruger: 'It is our country you want.' And, on 12 October 1899, war it was.

Children confront the camera in the Aliwal North concentration camp. The camps, part of Kitchener's 'scorched earth' policy, claimed the lives of nearly 30,000 Boers, most of them children, and an uncounted number of black South Africans who were held in separate camps. Almost all died of disease.

independent burgher state by sheer force of numbers. Johannesburg's *uitlanders*, for their part, began to demand the privileges of citizenship, reasonably at first, then vociferously, and finally violently.

By 1895 the confrontation between the restive English-speaking community, led by a group of mining magnates who called themselves the Reform Committee, on the one hand, and an ageing president determined to maintain the Transvaal's Afrikaner identity on the other, had grown to crisis proportions. Then, early on Monday 31 December, Dr Leander Starr Jameson and his raiding column of some 700 mounted troops from Rhodes's

Most people in Britain, Europe and the United States expected hostilities to last a few weeks. In fact it took more than two years for the best of the Empire's regiments, almost half a million men altogether, to subdue the rough-and-ready burgher commandos of the Transvaal and Orange Free State.

The Boers had very much the upper hand during the first month or two, notching up resounding victories at Colenso, Stormberg and Magersfontein within the space of a few days, a period that became known to the Imperial forces as 'British Black Week'. They went on to besiege the key garrison towns of Mafeking, Kimberley and Ladysmith; on the eastern flank, the brilliant young general Louis Botha rolled up the railway line deep into Natal. But numbers, and greater resources, were eventually to tell. Redvers Buller finally managed to breach the Tugela line, relieving Ladysmith on 28 February 1900. Lord Roberts and his chief-of-staff Kitchener pushed through the central front, occupying Johannesburg in May and Pretoria in June of the same year. It all seemed to be over bar the mopping up.

But the war was to drag on for another 23 long months, to cost tens of thousands of lives, and to devastate the northern territories.

Boer commandos under such enterprising leaders as Louis Botha, Christiaan de Wet, Jan Smuts and J.B.M. Hertzog took to the open veld, adopted hit-and-run tactics, and struck repeatedly at the enemy's communications, supplies and outlying garrisons. Against this rapier Kitchener, who was now in command, used the broadsword of blockhouse (over 8,000 of them) and barbed wire, scorched earth and concentration camp. Thirty thousand farmsteads were destroyed, whole villages burnt to the ground. Deneys Reitz, Boer soldier and son of a former Free State president, described a 'driven' area he passed through, 'leaving behind only blackened ruins and trampled fields, so that our course lay through a silent, unpeopled waste, across which we navigated our wagon like a lonely ship at sea'.

The women and children and black labourers of the Boer farming areas were rounded up in their thousands and incarcerated in camps that were designed to intern, not to exterminate. Nevertheless, over 27,000 whites, 22,000 of them children, died, mainly of disease, which spread like bush-fire in the overcrowded, unhygienic conditions. The scorching of the land, and the concentration camps, left a legacy that was to haunt two generations of white South Africans.

It would also be engraved on the collective memory of black South Africa. Wrote one observer towards the end: 'Of all who have suffered by the war, those who have endured the most and will receive the least sympathy, are the [blacks] of the country areas of the Transvaal ...'. The African communities suffered massive disruption, and profound injustice. It is thought that some 30,000 black folk, mainly the servants of Boer farmers, perished in the camps; most were simply dumped in enclosures on the open veld, without shelter or indeed, in many cases, without food.

Moreover, although the two combatants had at first tacitly agreed to keep the war an all-white affair, the British began recruiting black men as scouts and in other military capacities, and in due course arming them. Tens of thousands served under the Imperial flag, many were especially targeted and shot by the Boers, who regarded them as neutrals turned enemies. The killings reinforced the mutual suspicion and hostility that was to divide African and Afrikaner for the rest of the twentieth century.

Finally, the Boers in the field came to terms. On 15 May 1902, at a convention in Vereeniging, their leaders decided to negotiate. On 31 May, after nine days of hard bargaining, the two sides signed the Peace of Vereeniging at Melrose House, Pretoria. The terms were generous to the Boers: although the treaty returned their republics to the colonial fold, they were nevertheless guaranteed eventual self-government. Vereeniging also recognized Boer property rights, safeguarded the Dutch language, promised relief to war victims – and effectively denied black South Africans their political rights.

Indeed it had been a white man's war all along, and in the end it was a white man's peace.

RECONSTRUCTION AND UNION

Curiously, it was the architect of war, Lord Alfred Milner, who was to become chief engineer of South Africa's post-war recovery. His aims were to repair the ravaged land and resettle the denuded areas; to bring the mines back into operation; to create a customs union, and to consolidate the peace – in fact, to build a new (all-white) nation. Economic recovery, he believed, would heal the wounds of war, win back the goodwill of Transvaler and Free Stater. He exercised extreme diplomacy in his dealings with bloody but unbowed Afrikanerdom, publicly praising the Boers' 'patriotism, their courage, their resourcefulness, their endurance, their dignity and self-restraint in victory and their stoicism in defeat'.

Behind these splendid and sincere words, though, lurked the old Milner: his brave new world was to be an Anglo-Saxon one. His schemes included the settlement of 10,000 English-speaking farmers on the Highveld grasslands of the Transvaal 'within a twelve-month'; and in government schools 'Dutch should be used to teach English and English everything else'.

Milner's policy of anglicization met strong resistance from the Afrikaners. The recovery programme, on the other hand, succeeded beyond the expectations of even the most optimistic. To help get the economic wheels turning again, Milner gathered around him a group of talented young Oxford graduates – lawyers, administrators, economists: men such as Patrick Duncan (later Governor-General of South Africa); Lionel Curtis, author of the crucial *Selborne Memorandum*; Philip Kerr (who was to become British Ambassador to Washington); Geoffrey Dawson (future editor of the *Johannesburg Star* and of *The Times* of London); and John Buchan, the Lord Tweedsmuir (the famed novelist and later Governor-General of Canada). They became known as 'Milner's kindergarten' and contributed brilliantly to the process of reconstruction.

Central to this process were the gold mines which, at the time, were suffering from a critical shortage of labour. African workers, scattered by the winds of war, were slow to return from the outlying regions. Milner decided on indentured Chinese labour, the first of whom arrived on the Reef in 1904; over 60,000 followed, and the issue became highly controversial both in South Africa and Britain. By 1910 all had been repatriated – but they had served their purpose: the mines began generating wealth from mid-decade on.

There was progress, too, in the other economic sectors: most of the Boers were back on their lands by the end of 1902; a railway line was constructed between Kimberley and the Witwatersrand; another linked the Natal and Orange River Colony systems. A subcontinental customs union came into being in 1903.

Meanwhile there was a great deal of activity on the political front. Het Volk, a Transvaal Afrikaner organization led by ex-generals Botha and Smuts, started lobbying for second-language and other sectional rights in 1905. In the Orange River Colony, there was the similar Oranje Unie Afrikaner party. In due course both groups opened their membership lists to English-speakers; each won a resounding victory in elections to the legislatures of the self-governing colonies, both of which had been constituted in 1907.

Wider concepts, however, were taking hold of men's imaginations: first, political federation; then unification. Jan Smuts summed up the vision: 'What we want,' he said, 'is a supreme national authority to give expression to the national will of South Africa, and the rest is really subordinate.'

Political leaders in three territories and the white electorates of all four were in fact strongly in favour of Union (Natal's politicians were not, but voters in the referendum of 1908 gave an overwhelming mandate to the unionists). A national convention deliberated the issue between October 1908 and May 1909,

and most of its recommendations were incorporated into the Act of Union of 1909. On 31 May of the following year, the four colonies became one country, independent, with dominion status on the not-too-distant horizon. The Westminster system was adopted, comprising two parliamentary chambers (the senate acting in a largely advisory capacity), a cabinet of 10, four provincial authorities with considerable local powers, and a governor-general representing the Crown. The form of government was to remain virtually unchanged until South Africa became a republic in 1961.

Crucially, blacks were excluded from the democratic process – an omission which Milner would have regretted and, had he been able to, would have made good. A product of the classical Imperial school, brilliant, paternalistic, even-handed by inclination despite his 'betrayal' of the pre-war peace process, he believed sincerely in racial equality and in the gradual advancement of blacks towards political emancipation. But he had other and what seemed at the time more pressing priorities, and to meet them he needed the goodwill and active co-operation of both Boers and English-speakers. On matters of race his hands were tied. His one concession to what later became the central issue was the appointment, in 1903, of the Native Affairs Commission, which

MILNER'S AIMS WERE TO REPAIR THE **RAVAGED LAND**, RESETTLE THE DENUDED AREAS – AND BUILD A NEW (ALL-WHITE) **NATION**

Cape Town celebrates Union in 1910. British military victory, and the peace that followed, yielded little of comfort for the black peoples: they had not been invited to the unification talks, and they would be excluded from the democratic process for the next eight decades.

was headed by Sir Godfrey Lagden and composed of English-speaking whites only.

In retrospect and in terms of future race relations, the Lagden Commission was a total disaster. Its monumental report, produced two years later, was based on the premise that whites were of 'superior intellect', and it recommended, among much else, the formal separation of the races, the establishment of 'locations' for urban blacks, and the creation of reserves which roughly corresponded with the existing 'tribal homelands' of the Xhosa, Zulu and Sotho peoples. The document would be used by succeeding generations of white politicians to justify a growing arsenal of coercive, repressive and divisive laws based on race.

In short, very little was done for black South Africans following the Anglo-Boer War – a period of potentially progressive British rule. The wasted years proved crucial for the future. During the deliberations of the National Convention the Transvaal and Orange Free State delegates dug in their heels. Having successfully kept blacks out of the democratic process in their own republics, they were not about to bow to the liberal pretensions of colonies that allowed people of colour the vote, albeit a cosmetic one.

In fact only the Cape leadership – W.P. Schreiner, John X. Merriman and the enlightened Afrikaner François Malan – really pushed for the inclusion of blacks in the future constitutional arrangement. They demanded a 'civilization test' in which property, income and education were the criteria rather than race, and which would enfranchise some blacks and disenfranchise some whites. They received only lukewarm support from the Natal leadership and the British officials, and their efforts were only modestly rewarded: they extracted reluctant agreement to the retention of existing, very limited black voting rights until such time as the Union parliament should decide otherwise, as well as the constitutional entrenchment of the 'coloured vote' in the Cape and the right of coloured people to seek election to the Cape Provincial Council.

Significant, too, was the equal status accorded, within the constitution, to the Dutch and English languages. This was a major victory for those Afrikaners who had fought long and hard for all that it represented – Afrikaner identity and the emergence of Afrikanerdom as a coherent national political force.

GROWTH, CHANGE AND POLARIZATION

The years between Union in 1910 and the crucial parliamentary election of 1948 witnessed South Africa's transition from an uneven patchwork of colonial territories to a modern industrial nation. They were also years of war, of profound social change, and of complex political interaction, probably better summarized by broad themes than in chronological sequence.

Leaders of the South African Native National Congress (later renamed the African National Congress), formed in 1912. John Dube, the first president, sits at centre; celebrated author Sol Plaatje stands at right.

THE POLITICAL ARENA was dominated, throughout the entire span, by three Afrikaners, each of whom had served as a skilled military commander during the Anglo-Boer War.

Louis Botha held the Union premiership until his death in 1919, when the reins passed to Jan Smuts, his close associate and natural successor. Both were statesmen rather than politicians, both believed in conciliation between the two white cultural groups in South Africa; both were 'Empire men' in the sense that they valued close links with the former colonial power, each leading the country to war against Germany in support of Britain.

The third general, J.B.M. (Barry) Hertzog, was cast in an entirely different mould: a passionate republican and nationalist, he was determined to entrench Afrikaner power, though towards the end of his political career he was obliged to compromise in the interest of political expediency.

Throughout the tortuous political manoeuvrings of the 1920s and 1930s Smuts and Hertzog occupied centre stage, most of the time in direct opposition to each other but actually coming together in 1933, during the depths of the Great Depression, to form a coalition cabinet with Hertzog as prime minister. At the end of the following year their former parties were fused under the umbrella of the United Party and the two leaders directed the affairs of an increasingly prosperous country until the outbreak of the Second World War in September 1939, when Hertzog, anti-British to the last, resigned.

Some Afrikaner nationalists, the hardline conservatives, had refused to follow Hertzog's lead in 1934. Instead, they formed their own Reunited (*Herenigde*) National Party under the leadership of Cape clergyman and newspaper editor Daniël François Malan. Smuts, preoccupied with world events during the war and in the years immediately afterwards, badly underestimated the grassroots appeal – among voters of both white language groups – of a movement whose doctrinal cornerstone was apartheid, and at the 1948 general election his United Party paid the price.

THE YEARS OF WAR On two occasions during the twentieth century South African troops took to the battlefield in support of the country's Western allies.

Before marching into German South West Africa in 1915, Prime Minister Louis Botha was obliged to quell a full-scale insurrection at home. Memories of the concentration camps and the burning farms were still bitter among many Afrikaners; little more than a decade before, their men had been fighting for survival in their own valleys and veld, and now they were being asked to join 'the enemy' in a wider struggle. Altogether, some 11,000 burghers, led by Christiaan de Wet and other former guerrilla heroes, rose against their government in the traditional Boer 'armed protest'; one large commando, situated near the South West African (now Namibian) border, defected to the Germans. But the rebels enjoyed too little support in the country as a whole, and the uprising was short-lived: by the beginning of 1915 they had been scattered by disciplined government troops; most of their leaders were arrested and imprisoned and one was condemned and executed. (Another had drowned in the Vaal River.)

Botha could now turn his attention to the real enemy. He personally led a 12,000-man force from Swakopmund, Smuts another from Lüderitz Bay on the western coast; other columns marched in from the Orange River. The terrain was vast, and hostile, but the German-occupied garrison small, and by mid-July it was all over. Observed *The Times* of London: 'To the youngest of the sister nations belongs the glory of the first complete triumph of our arms and the disappearance of Germany from the map of Africa.' In the long run, though, the new occupation scarcely

proved a blessing, certainly not to the international community. Administered by South Africa as a mandate of the League of Nations from 1920, renamed Namibia by the United Nations in 1968, the territory became a source of constant international dispute until Namibian independence in 1990.

Other South African theatres of operation in the First World War were East Africa and the European western front. In both, the Union forces fought with distinction. Smuts, commander-in-chief of the Imperial army in Africa, executed a long and ultimately successful campaign in the east against the elusive German general Paul Emil von Lettow-Vorbeck. Bloodier by far were the battles in Flanders' fields. In one, at Delville Wood in July 1916, 121 officers and 3,032 men of the South African Brigade held their positions against massive bombardment and counter-attack for almost a week, the unwounded survivors numbering just five officers and 750 men.

Once again, in 1939, there was controversy over South Africa's obligations. But Jan Smuts – soldier, statesman, scholar, friend of both Winston Churchill and Mohandas Gandhi, member of the

One of thousands of black soldiers who served with the South African forces in the Western Desert. Many were captured when the fortress of Tobruk fell.

Jan Smuts, one of three brilliant Boer guerrilla commanders who occupied centre stage in the Union in the between-war years.

Imperial War Cabinet and loyalist (he was one of the prime architects of the Statute of Westminster which, in 1931, proclaimed the Commonwealth of Nations) – carried the parliamentary vote by 80 to 67. Opposition continued throughout the war, its active instrument the underground *Ossewabrandwag*. Generally speaking, though, the opponents of involvement were very much in the minority; whites of both language groups volunteered for active service in large numbers, as did black and coloured soldiers.

South African troops joined battle against Nazi Germany and its allies, again in East Africa (inflicting a stunning defeat on Mussolini's Italian forces in Abyssinia), in the Western Desert and in Europe, slogging their way up the spine of Italy in one of the hardest and most thankless campaigns of the war.

ECONOMIC GROWTH Exploitation of the Witwatersrand goldfields triggered the move, from the early years of the twentieth century, towards industrialization, and by definition urbanization – developments that changed the face of South Africa. Primary industry created the base for an impressive superstructure of heavy secondary industries, most notable of the early ones being ISCOR, the massive, initially state-controlled corporation which processes local iron and coal reserves to produce (and export) steel. ISCOR came on stream in 1934. The mining industry expanded steadily throughout the century, providing a solid base for the increasingly sophisticated manufacturing sector. Two global wars and a world greedy for South Africa's abundant raw materials and processed goods reinforced the impetus.

At the same time periodic drought, depression and new, labour-efficient farming techniques were forcing small farmers and tenants (*bywoners*) off the land and into the cities in droves. The 'poor white' problem was first identified as early as 1890; the Transvaal Indigency Commission reported a few years later that tens of thousands of refugees from the country areas were living 'in wretched shanties on the outskirts of towns', where they competed – largely unsuccessfully – with the low-earning black labour being drawn into the industrial system. In 1931 a Carnegie Corporation-funded investigation revealed that, of a white South African population of some 1.8 million, more than 300,000 had to be classed as 'very poor'.

This was at the depth of the Great Depression, and things would get better. Large-scale government assistance schemes, increasing prosperity, organized skills training and the growing manufacturing sector absorbed more and more white labour, and by the end of the 1930s, according to one historian, 'the poor white problem had virtually ceased to exist'. It did, however, leave a painful legacy, especially within official labour policy: the state would borrow from socialism to become the major employer, and job reservation would impose its artificial controls until the 1970s.

A poor white family of the 1930s. During this time, drought and the Depression forced tens of thousands of whites off the land and into a jobless life in the cities.

South Africa's labour relations story is not an especially happy one. Strikes and unrest were a depressingly regular feature of the industrial scene throughout the decades after Union. Most convulsive was the so-called 'red revolt' in 1922. In January of that year 22,000 Witwatersrand miners and engineering and power-station workers went on strike and organized themselves into paramilitary commandos, which were soon enough infiltrated by Marxist activists bent on a workers' revolution. Pitched battle broke out; troops were mobilized; 153 people (including 72 of the state forces) were killed, 534 wounded.

This particular upheaval gave graphic point to one of the constants in the social and economic history of modern South Africa: white fear of black encroachment. Times were hard in the 1920s and '30s, black labour extremely cheap (miners earned 2s 2d a day). It was publicly estimated that if 50 per cent of the white labour force could be replaced by blacks the mines would save £1 million a year, a huge amount in those days. Mine managements knew the facts; so did the unions, and the barricades went up as soon as it was announced, in December 1921, that 2,000 semi-skilled white gold-miners would be declared redundant.

Black urbanization, naturally, ran parallel to white. A new proletariat, officially regarded as 'temporary' and composed in part of tens of thousands of migrants from adjacent territories, collected in the enormous, controlled townships that began to mushroom around the mining and industrial centres of the Reef, Natal and the eastern Cape from the first years of the century.

It was largely in response to these pressures that successive Union governments expanded the body of discriminatory law. Among the more infamous measures were:

• **The Mines and Works Act (1911)**, which formalized job reservation by excluding blacks, on the grounds of competency, from numerous categories of skilled work both within the mining sector and on the railways.

• **The Natives' Land Act (1913)**, which confirmed the status of existing 'tribal' lands and set aside some seven per cent of the country for exclusive black occupation, much of it in present-day KwaZulu-Natal and the Ciskei and Transkei regions of the Eastern Cape. Within its terms blacks were prohibited from buying land elsewhere, a right they had previously enjoyed in the Cape and Natal.

• **The Native Affairs Act (1920)**, which made provision for separate community-based, government-appointed councils to represent the interests of blacks. The measure, refined in 1936 by the Representation of Natives Act, is considered a milestone in the history of segregation.

• **The Natives (Urban Areas) Act of 1923**, probably the most far-reaching piece of race control legislation of the period. The statute legally defined and established peri-urban locations, and gave white local authorities the power to exclude blacks from 'white' areas – and even from the locations themselves (when, for example, a resident was judged to be a vagrant or 'surplus to labour requirements'). This measure paved the way for the bedrock Group Areas Act of the later apartheid years, for mass forced removals and for the increasingly harsh application of the pass laws. And in its provision for the separate financing of township facilities (largely from the sale of beer), it also foreshadowed the Reservation of Separate Amenities Act, the ultimate agent of 'petty apartheid'.

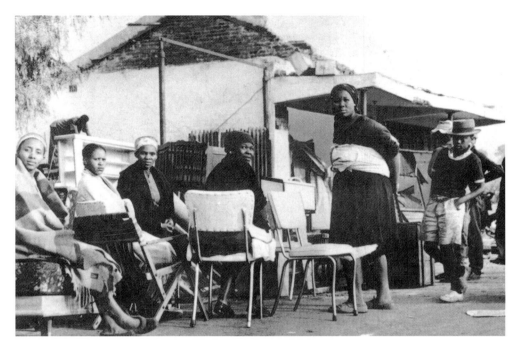

The brutal apartheid laws of the 1950s, which had their official origins in the first two decades of the century, enabled officialdom to force whole communities from their homes and into vast, sterile townships designated as 'Bantu' and other race-defined areas. One such casualty was Cape Town's District Six, another was Sophiatown, a run-down but vibrant Johannesburg suburb renowned for the number and quality of its artists, writers and musicians. Here, Sophiatown women wait for their houses to be destroyed (*left*); graffiti expresses brave defiance (*left bottom*).

THE **URBAN AREAS ACT** GAVE WHITE LOCAL AUTHORITIES THE **POWER** TO EXCLUDE BLACKS FROM **'WHITE' AREAS**

• **The Industrial Conciliation Act (1924)**, which excluded most black trade unions from the collective bargaining process. Its intent was reinforced by the second Act, of 1937, which in addition reserved certain occupations for apprentice-trained workers. There were no black apprentices at the time.

• **The Native Administration Act (1927)**, an attempt to give some sort of national coherence to 'native policy'. For the first time, blanket executive power was vested in a central Native Affairs Department, which rapidly became an autocratic, all-powerful and largely unaccountable 'state within a state'.

• **The Immorality Act (1927)**, which prohibited extramarital sexual relations between black and white, though for the time being marriages across the colour line remained legal.

• **The Native Trust Land Act (1936)**, passed after the Beaumont Commission reported serious overcrowding and degradation in the 'homelands'. This consolidated the legislation of 1913, extending the areas reserved for black people to 13 per cent of the country.

THE VICTORY OF AFRIKANERDOM

By the end of the Second World War the 'poor white' problem had largely been eradicated; the white unemployed and unemployables of the 1930s had become the working class of the 1940s. The old fears, though, were still there. In 1946 just over 40 per cent of Afrikaner working males were in manual or unskilled occupations, 32 per cent were on the land, and only 27 per cent held white-collar jobs. The war years had galvanized industry, prompting a growing demand for black labour and skills; job reservation came under pressure; increasing mechanization threatened the traditionally white artisan class, both English- and Afrikaans-speaking; and demobilization and post-war immigration brought a new edge to competition in the workplace. Smuts's ever more liberal statements on race added to the general climate of insecurity among white wage-earners.

So, too, did the Fagan Commission's findings, released in February 1948. A conservative document by later standards, the report nevertheless stated that segregation was 'totally impracticable', that urban drift was inevitable, and that large black communities were now a permanent feature of the country's human and economic landscape, should be accepted as such and, indeed, actually brought a degree of stability to the labour market.

The National Party's (HNP's) own commission, led by ideologue Paul Sauer, produced different (and, for anxious whites, far more comforting) conclusions. Malan capitalized on the insecurities. He focused on the colour question, promising to retain the exclusive white vote, halt racial integration at all levels, safeguard white jobs and privilege within the framework of a supremacist master-plan.

The assurances fell on fertile ground and the National Party, with the crucial co-operation of Nicolaas Havenga's small Afrikaner Party, won the watershed 1948 election, squeezing into power with a majority of five seats. In May 1948 D.F. Malan took office to form South Africa's first all-Afrikaner government.

Nationalist prime minister, Daniël Malan (more commonly known as D.F. Malan), leader of the country's first all-Afrikaner government which came to power in 1948, speaks to his race-obsessed supporters.

THE SOCIAL ENGINEERS

The National Party remained in power for more than 40 years, though its position in parliament was tenuous enough to start with. In order to consolidate its dominance, not only over the black people but also over the English-speaking United Party opposition, Malan needed total control over parliament and, crucially, over the public service.

The first requirement – an overwhelming parliamentary majority – would have to wait for the 1954 general election, but in the meantime, the Nationalists calculated, much could be done to strengthen their power base in the country at large. The first, critical, stage was the process of 'Afrikanerization', which began immediately, with a deceptively reasonable insistence that all government employees would henceforth have to be bilingual. Those civil servants who could not speak Afrikaans would be replaced by Afrikaners familiar with English. At the same time

there were wholesale sackings and early retirements and, before long, senior and middle-echelon positions in every branch of the administration, armed forces and police were filled by those whose loyalties to party and *volk* were unquestioned.

During the first two decades the formal division, or stratification, along racial lines provided the thrust of policy. But, if the new regime was to succeed in parcelling the country up into racial segments, it first needed to define race. This it attempted to do with the passage of the Population Registration Act in 1950 and a series of enabling laws during the following years. All these reduced down to a crude formula which held physical appearance (colour), customary association and 'repute' to be the characteristics distinguishing one race from another.

From these measures flowed all else, including a racially based identity document (which, when refined over time, provided a razor-sharp instrument of control) and, most notably, that massive foundation of apartheid, the Group Areas Act. The latter, linchpin of a draconian and wide-ranging legislative pro-gramme, was designed to confine each race to its own residential and trading areas. A logical extension of Group Areas was the later (1953) Reservation of Separate Amenities Act, a measure which, together with the regulations that followed, segregated a variety of facilities ranging from public buildings and transport to such ordinary community comforts as parks and libraries, beaches, benches and entertainment. The 'whites only' signs went up in their millions. Further statutes included those restricting freedom of movement, regulation of the workplace, and an arsenal of security laws.

All this, as we have seen, was not especially new: the ingredients of the southern African melting pot had never really melted. They were kept apart, from the early colonial days, by competition, by perhaps irreconcilable cultural distinctions, by fierce informal pressures and by formal edict. But from 1950 there were both qualitative and quantitative differences. Now, for the first time, Afrikanerdom was in the national driving seat, and for the first time rigid segregation was entrenched within an all-embracing legal code and structured administration.

There were laws, too, affecting the coloured people. In 1951 the Separate Registration of Voters Act, designed to remove coloured voters from the common roll (they were to be represented in parliament by four white Members) was passed but subsequently declared invalid by the Appellate Division of the Supreme Court. Five controversial years later, however, and after a startling series of constitutional acrobatics, the Act became effective. In 1969 the last vestiges of coloured parliamentary

The divided society: apartheid laws deny black South Africans such ordinary comforts as park benches, this one being reserved for 'Europeans only'.

FOR USE BY WHITE PERSONS

THESE PUBLIC PREMISES AND THE AMENITIES THEREOF HAVE BEEN RESERVED FOR THE EXCLUSIVE USE OF WHITE PERSONS.

By Order   Provincial Secretary

THE REPUBLIC

Significantly, D.F. Malan, just before he assumed office, supported the granting to India of a republican constitution within the Commonwealth. The Nationalists, chafed by the tenuous but irritating Imperial bonds that were the legacy of Union and dominion status, aspired to the same freedom, and the issue was openly broached by Hendrik Verwoerd in the early months of 1960 (British premier Harold Macmillan's 'winds of change' address to the joint Houses of Parliament in Cape Town – in which he gave implicit notice that Britain would abandon her responsibilities in Africa and elsewhere, confer independence on her remaining colonies, and turn her face towards Europe instead – reinforced an already strong resolve to cut the ties). A referendum was held later in the year at which the electorate, by a modest majority of 74,580 votes, decided in favour of a republican form of government.

In the interim serious unrest had broken out in parts of the country, the culmination of sporadic riots that had started the year before in protest against the enforced carrying of reference books (passes) and largely orchestrated by the Pan-Africanist Congress. On 21 March 1960 police confronted a large crowd in the township of Sharpeville, near Vereeniging in the Transvaal; shots were fired; 69 blacks were killed and hundreds wounded. There were also riots and, soon afterwards, massive protest marches in Cape Town. The PAC and its big brother, the African National Congress, were banned. A state of emergency was declared.

Sharpeville was a seminal event. Before the shootings the country, for all the criticism directed at it, was accepted as a member of the international community; after March 1960 it faced increasing isolation. Exactly a year later Verwoerd flew to London to apply for continued Commonwealth membership of a republican South Africa. Harsh words were exchanged at the conference; South Africa withdrew its application; two months later the Republic was formally established.

Hendrik Verwoerd, Dutch-born and Rhodesian-educated, doctrinaire, brilliant, ruthless and uncompromising, died on 6 September 1966, victim of an assassin's knife (the killer was a parliamentary messenger, subsequently adjudged unfit to stand trial). Verwoerd had been the chief architect of separate development, designing and constructing a monolithic structure that would become the increasingly sharp focus of critical attention, both nationally and internationally. It would also present his successors with possibly the toughest of political, and moral, challenges.

representation ended, to be replaced by the partly elected, partly nominated Coloured Persons Representative Council (CRC).

It was the status and future of the black people, however, that preoccupied the Nationalist government. Under Malan and his successors – J.G. Strijdom (1954–1958) and, especially, Hendrik Verwoerd (1958–1966) – the policy of enforced segregation was carried to its logical and lunatic extremes. In its simplest form, the argument held that the blacks had their own, traditional territories and that it was in these that they should exercise the legitimate rights of citizenship and the vote. The long, laborious process of creating separate black states began in a modest way with the Black Authorities Act of 1951 (it set up tribal, regional and territorial authorities *within* the Union of South Africa), and reached its legislative zenith in 1959 with the Promotion of Black Self-Government Act. This provided for the establishment of homelands (later known as national states) for the country's main black groups, and for the development in these territories of governmental institutions which would eventually lead, in each case and by predetermined stages, to full independence.

Silent lines of mourners pay their respects to those killed at Sharpeville. The 1960 massacre of 69 people who had been protesting against the stringent pass laws was a watershed event in the long and dismal story of apartheid.

DIALOGUE AND PROTEST

The man who succeeded Verwoerd, B.J. Vorster, was also a hardline conservative, but a pragmatic one who perceived the dangerous long-term consequences of isolation and the need to establish 'normal and friendly relations' with African states (in fact Verwoerd had also recognized the realities, but too late to translate conviction into effective action).

The Republic was an African country, the most powerful south of the Sahara; some states were economically dependent on it; the whole complex of southern African nations economically inter-dependent. This was the era of détente and dialogue, and a significant degree of rapprochement, or at least of contact, was achieved. A flurry of diplomatic activity in the late 1960s and 1970s produced some positive results: Malawi established formal links with Pretoria; closer ties were forged with Lesotho, Botswana and Swaziland; the South African premier paid successful goodwill visits to Malawi (1969), the Ivory Coast (1974) and Liberia (1975). There were reciprocal courtesies: Vorster met Zambia's Kenneth Kaunda at the Victoria Falls in 1975 in a joint effort to solve the thorny problem of Rhodesia's rebellion (the country had unilaterally declared its independence from Britain in November 1965, an act which polarized racial opinion and inhibited the whole détente exercise). In the end it was Vorster who, with Henry Kissinger, the United States secretary of state, was instrumental in bringing Rhodesian leader Ian Smith to the negotiating table.

Farther afield, however, the story was by no means one of unqualified success. On the contrary, South Africa's relations with the international community, with countries beyond her immediate sphere of influence, continued to deteriorate. Criticism of South Africa's internal arrangements mounted at the United Nations; the Carter administration's Andrew Young (a leading civil-rights activist and the US representative to the United Nations) stirred the hitherto distracted American liberal conscience; a militarily successful but diplomatically disastrous incursion into Marxist Angola (responsibility was as much Washington's as Pretoria's) helped fix the international spotlight on what was seen as a 'destabilization' policy and on the intractable question of Namibian independence.

Nor was all quiet on the home front. In June 1976 unrest erupted in the huge, sprawling township of Soweto near Johannesburg and spread to other centres, continuing in varying degrees of intensity for almost eight months. The subsequent commission of inquiry found that the immediate cause was the use of Afrikaans as a teaching medium in black high schools. General discrimination, lack of citizenship, restrictions on property ownership and lack of civic facilities were powerful contributory factors. The riots, however, were not spontaneous incidents, but rather part of a sustained, organized campaign, launched by a number of black consciousness organizations, to undermine the social order. In October 1977 the Government banned 17 of these bodies together with many of their leaders.

OPPOSING FORCES

The origin of the South African extra-parliamentary opposition movements – if one discounts the lone voices of late nineteenth-century black intellectuals such as Tiyo Soga and John Tengo Jabavu – are properly to be found in the years of disenchantment following the Anglo-Boer War. British 'non-racial justice', anticipated when the two northern territories returned to colonial rule, did not materialize, and a number of black congress-type associations made their appearance (the Vigilance Association in the eastern Cape and Transkei territory; the South African Native Congress in the western Cape; the Natal Native Congress, and the Transvaal Congress). Such bodies, although vocal, were ineffective.

Nor did blacks have a say in the deliberations that created the Union of South Africa in 1910 (*see* page 36). Despite strenuous representations to the British constitution-makers, the future was shaped without consultation with blacks. But in 1912 they combined, under the leadership of Durban lawyer Pixley Seme, to form the South African Native National Congress, a body renamed the African National Congress in 1925.

He returned to India in 1914 to work long, hard and ultimately triumphantly for that country's independence from Britain.

The history of the black opposition movement – that is to say, of the African National Congress in particular, although workers' and religious organizations were active and articulate in the between-war years – is a complicated narrative. Organized resistance to the steady erosion of black human and political rights remained remarkably moderate through the first half of the twentieth century – partly because it was slow to become a mass movement in the modern sense of the term. The disenfranchised urban African communities were too economically deprived, too impermanent and, above all, too demoralized by the growing arsenal of segregationist laws to provide a strong enough power base for the leadership. And the movement was anything but a unified whole: the ANC was just one of a number of articulate and non-violent political, labour and church (largely of the charismatic kind) bodies active in the era between the wars. Indeed for a time it was quite overshadowed by the giant Industrial and Commercial Union (ICU), founded in 1919 by the Malawian, Clements Kadalie, and which in 1927 boasted more than 100,000 members.

Over the years the ANC retained its liberal expectations, but eventually turned to a mild form of militancy – passive resistance. Attitudes had hardened as the 1940s progressed: in 1944 Prime Minister Smuts refused to receive a million-signature protest petition delivered to the gates of parliament in Cape Town; there were clashes; ANC leaders were arrested. Two years later, 60,000 black mineworkers went on strike on the Rand for higher wages, better working conditions, union recognition and an end to the hugely destructive migrant labour system. The response from the government was to call in the police, round up the strikers and force them down the shafts at bayonet point. Twelve miners were killed, over a thousand injured. From then on, direct confrontation – well organized and strengthened by a new sense of unity among blacks – was to play an increasingly prominent part in the drawn-out struggle for human rights.

Thousands gather near Johannesburg in 1955 to endorse the Freedom Charter, a call by the oppressed for basic human rights, and among the century's most important documents for black South Africans in their struggle for dignity.

At about the same time, a talented Indian advocate was crusading, with some success, for Asian rights in South Africa. Mohandas K. Gandhi had arrived in Durban in 1893 to take up a private legal brief. He founded the Natal Indian Congress a year later and, after two decades of political confrontation (during which he was imprisoned twice), finally reached an accord with General Jan Smuts. It was during these years that Gandhi evolved his political philosophy and technique, *Satyagraha* – commonly termed 'passive resistance' but more literally 'keeping to the truth'.

The passive resistance phase abruptly came to an end with the enactment of the Criminal Law Amendment Bill in 1952, though the ANC still drew a line at the use of clandestine force: ANC president Chief Albert Luthuli, a Rhodesian-born Zulu aristocrat and churchman, was formally 'banned' in 1952 but his moral leadership – his rejection of violence – continued to be acknowledged by the majority of members. Luthuli was awarded the Nobel Peace Prize in 1961.

A new initiative, and the last major peaceful one for more than three decades, began on 26 June 1955. Some 3,000 delegates of all races attended the Congress of the People at Kliptown, near Johannesburg, to endorse the Freedom Charter, one of the most significant political statements of the South African century and heavily socialist in tone. It advocated a colour-blind approach to the country's problems and future, affirmed that South Africa belonged to all its inhabitants, and that no government could exercise authority save by the will of the people. Signatories at the time included the ANC, the South African Indian Congress, the South African Coloured People's Congress and the (white) Congress of Democrats.

Four months later police raided the homes of more than 500 activists, the prelude to a massive crackdown that saw thousands arrested, restricted or 'banned'. In December of the following year 156 people were imprisoned in Johannesburg Fort, preparatory to that most protracted of judicial sagas, the notorious Treason Trial. They had been arrested for their part in organizing the Kliptown Congress and its charter, which was deemed to be a communist document designed to overthrow the state; among them were Nelson Mandela, Walter Sisulu, Helen Joseph and Lilian Ngoyi. The charges were dismissed by the Supreme Court – five years later.

Towards the end of the decade serious divisions began to appear in the ranks of the ANC. The younger, more militant element was fast losing faith in a leadership that stressed the need for non-violent protest. Civil disobedience and boycotts had led nowhere; white nationalism was more firmly in the saddle than ever, and most of its opponents languished in prison or under house arrest.

The radicals within the organization – the so-called Africanists – rejected the Freedom Charter, seeking instead an exclusively black, revolutionary solution. In 1959, under the leadership of Robert Sobukwe, they broke away to form the Pan-Africanist Congress. A year later Sharpeville (*see* page 43) brought the rivalry between the two organizations into keen focus: each organization campaigned vigorously against the pass laws, urging township blacks to leave their reference (pass) books at home, invite arrest, and overload the entire security system.

On 28 March 1960 both the ANC and the PAC were banned in terms of the Unlawful Organisations Act, and went underground; some of its leaders, including Oliver Tambo, fled into exile. The ANC, on Nelson Mandela's initiative, formed its military wing, Umkonto we Sizwe ('spear of the nation'), and targeted 'hard' objectives: government installations, communications and so forth. Loss of life was to be avoided. Poqo, Umkonto we Sizwe's PAC counterpart, had more violent intent.

The sabotage campaign was waged until 1963, when police raided Umkhonto's operational headquarters at Lilliesleaf farm in

Rivonia, near Johannesburg. Most of its top leadership, together with a mountain of incriminating evidence, was seized. Those arrested *in situ* included Walter Sisulu, Govan Mbeki, Raymond Mhlaba and Ahmed Kathrada. Others were detained shortly afterwards, and among those finally brought to court was Mandela, who had been serving a five-year prison term for incitement.

The Rivonia Trial began in October 1963 and lasted seven months. The 10 accused pleaded guilty, eight receiving life sentences. From the dock, Mandela spelled out his vision. He had,

Treason trialists pose for a group photo: 156 were arrested in 1955; all were eventually acquitted, the last of them in 1961.

he said, dedicated himself to 'the struggle of the African people. I have fought against white domination, and I have fought against black domination. I have cherished the ideal of a democratic and free society in which all persons live together in harmony and with equal opportunities. It is an ideal for which I hope to live for … . But if needs be it is an ideal for which I am prepared to die.'

The arena, from the late 1960s and especially in the 1970s, became even more crowded. 'Black Consciousness' organizations, led by the younger breed, appeared on the scene. In June 1976 Soweto erupted in flames as students took to the streets *en masse* (*see* page 44). The riots, however, were not a spontaneous expression of popular discontent but part of a sustained campaign to undermine the social and political order. Prime movers were a number of university and other student bodies belonging to the Black People's Convention, an umbrella organization which gave some cohesion to various elements of the Black Consciousness Movement. The latter, founded by a young activist named Steve Biko, totally rejected white liberalism, urging blacks to take pride in their own capabilities and to rely only on themselves in the struggle for their rights.

In August 1977 Biko was arrested and held in police custody for 24 days before succumbing to brain injury after being driven to Pretoria in the back of a police vehicle. Biko's death, said Minister of Justice Jimmy Kruger, 'leaves me cold'. At the inquest, the police were absolved from blame; the three doctors connected with the case were also exonerated. A month later Kruger banned two newspapers and 17 organizations linked to the Black Consciousness Movement, and detained their leaders.

During the 1980s the African National Congress remained proscribed. Nelson Mandela and other key figures in the liberation struggle languished on Robben Island and in other prisons; and Oliver Tambo and his lieutenants in exile organized and operated a sophisticated external network, based in the Zambian capital Lusaka but also with an effective presence in Tanzania and other African countries, and with representation in major northern hemisphere centres. Internally, though, the political arena became increasingly polarized. There appeared to be little common ground for negotiation between the elected government and the disaffected extra-parliamentary opposition; the pressures built up; lawlessness intensified, the violence, which reached its crescendo in mid-decade, falling into two broad categories: sustained mob unrest, and sabotage.

A state of emergency covering 36 of South Africa's 260 magisterial districts was declared in 1985, extended shortly afterwards, then lifted in March 1986, only to be reimposed within weeks. This conferred on the minister of law and order and on the commissioner of police wide powers to arrest, detain, ban and otherwise regulate to preserve peace and security. The measures had their immediate effect – the incidence of violent unrest declined dramatically – but the emergency cost the country dearly in terms of adverse international publicity, loss of investor confidence and, above all, in terms of political progress.

P.W. BOTHA AND REFORM

The National Party celebrated its thirtieth year in office in 1978 – three decades during which racial separation had been sedulously entrenched.

That year, though, was to mark the start of a new era. In September, B.J. Vorster resigned as premier to become state president, and was replaced by former Minister of Defence P.W. Botha, a finger-wagging autocrat of the old school but, it seemed, a realist as well. These changes took place in the middle of what became known as the Information Scandal. Probes by the press, police and, later, the Erasmus Commission revealed that government funds had been misused by officials in the Department of Information, and that the prime minister of the time had known of the irregularities. Vorster resigned

the presidency. Also implicated was Dr Connie Mulder, former minister of information, who resigned his seat in the house.

The new premier made it clear from the outset that he was determined on a reformist course. The Information controversy delayed the initiative for almost a year, but in August 1979 Botha outlined a 12-point plan to the Natal congress of the National Party: his 'total strategy' for the security and gradual transformation of the social and political order. The plan included provision for power devolution, the recognition of the rights of ethnic groups, the consolidation of the homelands ('national states' and 'independent republics'), the creation of a 'constellation of southern African states', the removal of 'unnecessary discrimination', and, above all, a new constitutional dispensation (*see* page 50).

The most dramatic moves were on the labour front. Two commissions of inquiry, the Wiehahn and the Riekert, had together recommended the maximum use of all available skills and the removal of almost every law that discriminated against black workers. Government accepted most of the recommendations. Job reservation along racial lines had long been subject to natural erosion, the artificial barriers crumbling under the pressure of market forces. Now, with the active participation of the private sector, blacks were to be brought fully into the body economic through intensified training, integration and the elimination of the wage gap. Collective bargaining would in fact prove one of the keys to genuine advancement: black trade unions, fully recognized, would be the sharpest instrument in the operation to improve the lot of the urban black. In the event, the unions organized themselves with remarkable speed and expertise, giving the black workforce powerful economic and, potentially, political muscle almost overnight. In due course, other significant changes occurred in the urban context: black townsfolk achieved a more permanent status with the right to purchase homes on the long (99-year) lease and later, in many instances, to buy houses outright even though they were technically citizens of national states rather than citizens of the Republic of South Africa. Above all, influx control and the 'pass laws' were finally legislated out of existence in 1986, and a new and far less provocative system of identify documentation introduced.

However, the thrust of the Botha strategy was – had to be – in the constitutional field. The senate was abolished in 1980, signalling the demise of the Westminster system in South Africa. A new body, the President's Council, comprising 60 nominated coloured, Indian and white members, was established to investigate and recommend a new constitution. This it did, presenting its package in May 1982. The recommendations, which were accepted, made provision for an executive president, a parliament of three houses (white, Asian and coloured), a non-racial cabinet; a reconstituted President's Council; and changes, intended to accommodate some black political aspirations, at local and regional government level. Once again, though, black South Africans were excluded from the central process: they were still deemed to be citizens of one or another of the homelands. Botha announced that the proposals would be put to the test of a referendum to be held on 2 November 1983.

Among those who endorsed the proposals were the 'official' Indian bodies, and the Labour Party, for long a major voice of the coloured people and an opponent of established government. The endorsement shattered the credibility of these organizations, dissipating their traditional support.

Ranged against the scheme were parliamentary groups to the left (the Progressive Federal Party, led by Dr F. van Zyl Slabbert) and to the right (notably the Conservative Party). The Conservative leader, Dr Andries Treurnicht, had resigned his cabinet portfolio in 1982, and, together with ex-ministers Connie Mulder and Ferdinand Hartzenberg, had formed the party to fight what was perceived as a dangerous 'drift to the left'. Sixteen right-wing MPs joined the new organization, whose power base lay largely in the north of the country. Strong but voteless voices raised against the proposed tricameral system included those of KwaZulu's Chief Mangosuthu Buthelezi, all the liberation organizations, and the United Democratic Front (UDF), a popular mass-movement formed to campaign, legitimately, for a 'no' response.

In the event, the electorate gave overwhelming approval to the new constitution: 66 per cent voted in favour – a signal victory for P.W. Botha. The process of reform got under way during the first session of the new parliament; high points were the abolition of the Mixed Marriages Act and Section 16 of the Immorality Act. The real significance, though, was that whites and people of colour were for the very first time deliberating and legislating together, and that change was very much in the air. A wedge, feeble as yet, had been driven into the monolithic structure of institutionalized apartheid.

Coincident with all this was a sudden and deep economic recession, triggered originally by unfavourable commodity markets, a falling gold price and state over-spending; latterly by unrest, serious inflation, loss of banking and investor confidence and a decline in the value of the rand against the world's major currencies.

Ironically, or perhaps predictably, this was the time chosen by internal opponents and important sections of the international community to increase pressure for rapid and fundamental change. The disinvestment debate; sanctions; sporting isolation; township violence and the state of emergency occupied the headlines, and the regime retreated into laager. Over the months, the reform initiative became subordinate to the perceived need to counter extra-parliamentary opposition to the co-optive approach to government, and by the end of 1986 it was security rather than political progress that held centre stage.

SIGNS OF CHANGE

However, the outlook was not entirely gloomy. Even though the hardline Conservatives gained 22 of the parliamentary seats in the 1987 general election and came close to winning a dozen more, it was evident that the ruling National Party harboured a powerful progressive element within its ranks. Left-of-centre independents had also put up a remarkably strong showing at the polls. Clearly, a great many white South Africans did in fact want change.

Moreover, there were shortly to be significant moves towards regional détente. In 1988, under joint US-Soviet pressure, the parties involved in the Angolan-Namibian impasse met in Brazzaville (Republic of Congo), Cairo and other venues to negotiate Cuban withdrawal from the subcontinent, Namibian autonomy and a resolution of the Angolan civil war. The Brazzaville Protocol was signed in November of that year and confirmed in New York a month later, setting an April 1989 date for the formal start of the Namibian independence process. In March 1990 Namibia became a fully independent state, taking her place in the community of nations.

Meanwhile, talks had also been held with the Mozambican leadership; the succeeding months saw a marked improvement in relations between South Africa and Angola, and for the first time in a decade there was real hope of an end to the civil wars that had ravaged the former Portuguese territories, and which were bedevilling intra-regional relationships.

These events corresponded with the mood of the times. The wind of change was gusting throughout the world, sweeping away the values, priorities and assumptions of the old international order. The Russian empire was collapsing, bringing down the authoritarian regimes of Eastern Europe, and territorial competition between the major powers had ended. Southern Africa, of course, could not remain immune from the trends.

THE BREAKTHROUGH

In January 1989, President P.W. Botha suffered a mild stroke and, a few weeks later, resigned the leadership of the National Party in favour of Transvaal strongman F.W. de Klerk, who had generally been regarded as a hardline conservative.

Later, Botha also resigned the state presidency, after fighting a bitter and somewhat unseemly rearguard action – against senior politicians who were now agreed that the government's

Violence and counter-violence plagued South Africa's black townships during the 1980s as activists and their supporters sought 'to make the country ungovernable'. The pressures, both internal and external, eventually proved too much, bringing the regime to the negotiating table.

anti-communist 'Total Strategy' had become irrelevant, that the era of the 'securocrats' had passed, that apartheid was an anachronism, and that the time had come for an entirely new dispensation in South Africa. The changes that followed were rapid, fundamental, dramatic and far-reaching.

A general election in the latter part of 1989 confirmed that opinion within white society had polarized. The Nationalists lost ground to both the right and to a growing body of realists disenchanted with policies that seemed to be leading only to a nationwide state of anarchy. Time and circumstance favoured the moderates: pressures to release ANC leader Nelson Mandela, by now the world's best-known political prisoner, and to reach an accommodation with the black majority, had become irresistible.

At the opening session of the new parliament in February 1990, President de Klerk announced the unbanning of the ANC, the PAC, the South African Communist Party and a number of other proscribed organizations, and the release of political prisoners. Two weeks later Mandela, incarcerated for the previous 27 years (initially on Robben Island and later in the grounds of Victor Verster prison at Paarl, north-east of Cape Town), walked to freedom.

The decades of white political supremacy were over; the new South Africa, its shape as yet undefined, had been born.

FIRST STEPS

The journey towards political settlement and the establishment of a fully democratic order within South Africa was long, hard, and fraught with hazard. The events of 1990, the inaugural year of the new era, set the pattern.

One of De Klerk's first moves as president had been to dismantle P.W. Botha's National Security Management System, a sinister network that had effectively hijacked a large part of the civil authority. This was a major setback for the 'securocrats' – hard-nosed white conservatives, many of whom were believed to lurk in the middle and upper echelons of the police and armed forces and who were determined to sabotage reconciliation by any means, fair or (predominantly) foul, at their disposal.

Much of this covert campaign was allegedly concentrated within the curiously named Civil Co-operation Bureau (CCB), a hit squad which targeted political and human rights activists and which was thought to have arranged the assassinations of, among many, many others, the 'Cradock Four', campaigner Ruth First (by letter bomb), university academic David Webster, and the liberal Namibian lawyer Anton Lubowski. The Harms Commission of Inquiry, set up in January 1990, faced bureaucratic obstruction and was obliged to exonerate senior military men and politicians (including Minister of Defence Magnus Malan), but voiced strong suspicions that the CCB was involved in 'more crimes of violence than the evidence shows'.

On 13 September 1990, 26 people were shot and hacked to death and more than 100 injured in the first of many senseless 'train massacres' on the Johannesburg-Soweto line. Reactionary violence – promoted by an undefined but widely rumoured 'third force', and by other groups both to the left and right, each with vested interests in chaos – was to threaten the peace process for four long years. Nevertheless, there was encouraging progress. June 1990 saw the demise of the hated Separate Amenities Act, and within a year the whole body of apartheid legislation – including the cornerstone Population Registration Act, the Group Areas Act and laws that reserved 83 per cent of the country for whites – disappeared from the statute books.

Things were also moving on the international front. In September of the same year De Klerk travelled to the United States – on the first official visit of a South African government leader in 44 years – to extract a promise that sanctions would be lifted once the reform process was seen as 'irreversible'. In December, the European Community began the normalizing process by lifting the voluntary ban on new investments.

The ANC suspended its armed struggle, and on 13 December its president, Oliver Tambo, returned to his native country after an enforced absence of 30 years. Some 20,000 other political exiles were formally granted indemnity.

PAINFUL PROGRESS

Tentative talks between the government, the ANC and other organizations, which had started in 1990, continued through the following year. The leaders of 19 groups came together to inaugurate the Convention for a Democratic South Africa (Codesa) and to sign a keynote declaration of intent to construct a post-apartheid constitution 'by consensus' (effectively, by majority vote within the Convention). Codesa, it was agreed, would have law-making authority and, although the obsolescent three-chamber parliament would retain veto powers, the National Party government undertook to use its parliamentary majority to facilitate new legislation. Notable absentees from the forum, at least initially, were the Pan-Africanist Congress, which continued to maintain a revolutionary stance, and Zulu Chief Buthelezi's Inkatha Freedom Party.

The issues were complex, some of them seemingly intractable. De Klerk had, from the first, rejected simple majority rule in favour of a power-sharing formula that contained checks against the 'domination of one group by another', a euphemism for entrenching white minority rights. He also advocated federalism – the devolution of power from the centre to the regions. Conversely, the ANC and its partners wanted, among other things, a unitary state and a winner-takes-all electoral arrangement.

Both sides had their trump cards. The government could hold the whole process to ransom simply by stonewalling, and by giving covert support to Inkatha in its campaign for ethnic independence. The ANC, which desperately needed positive results (party rank and file, and the people of the townships, were growing increasingly restive), had immense popular backing and could summon up 'rolling mass action' in support of its demands. It was also prepared to use international sanctions as a bargaining counter.

In the event, the United States Congress, recognizing 'a profound transformation in South Africa', repealed the Comprehensive Anti-Apartheid Act in July 1991. In that year, too, South African athletes rejoined the Olympic movement and, though they performed with only moderate success, their presence at Barcelona a year later helped signal the passing of the wilderness years.

UPS AND DOWNS

Hopes of a political breakthrough were reinforced by the whites-only referendum held on 17 March 1992. The electorate was asked whether it supported the 'continuation of the reform process which the state president began on 2 February 1990, and which is aimed at a new constitution through negotiation', and a surprising 68.6 per cent of voters responded favourably. 'Today,' said De Klerk, 'we have closed the book on apartheid.'

But matters suddenly took a turn for the worse. The government delegation at Codesa, basking in the referendum's success and its own perceived position on the moral high ground, over-confident, even arrogant, overplayed its hand, and the talks were suspended.

Other setbacks occurred with depressing regularity, among them:

• The massacre of 45 innocents in the Transvaal township of Boipatong in June 1992 – a tragedy widely rumoured (but not proven) to be the work of the 'third force'. Evidence gathered by the respected Goldstone Commission later revealed a large-scale dirty tricks campaign sanctioned by senior military officers. A Human Rights Commission report estimated that 3,499 people died in political violence during 1992.

• The confrontation between ANC marchers and troops of the Ciskei army in September 1992. Thirty of the former were gunned down, more than 200 injured, and the negotiations placed in jeopardy. Mandela and De Klerk, however, moved quickly to defuse the crisis, signing a record of understanding which committed the parties to the creation of a non-racial transitional government followed by the democratic election of a constituent assembly.

• The assassination by maverick right-wingers, on 10 April 1993, of Chris Hani, general secretary of the South African Communist Party, member of the ANC's inner council and a hero to the young black radicals. Again, the will to make political progress won the day, and the talks proceeded.

• The continued intransigence of Chief Buthelezi and his Inkatha Freedom Party. The 'Zulu factor' was to prove a serious obstacle to settlement until well past the eleventh hour.

• Similarly, the obstructionist tactics of white conservatives intent on their own Volkstaat, or peoples' republic. The far-right fringe threatened civil war. The more moderate element, together with the governments of Ciskei and KwaZulu, applied pressure through a loosely constituted body known as the Concerned South Africans Group (Cosag), later renamed the Freedom Alliance.

THE LAST MILE

In December 1993 parliament was effectively superseded by a multi-party Transitional Executive Council (TEC), the product of a negotiation process that had started in earnest two full years before. It convened in terms of an agreement, reached by Codesa's successor in June 1993, on an interim constitution, on the reincorporation of the homelands, and on a date for national elections.

The polls, scheduled for the following April, were to be held on the basis of universal adult suffrage and proportional representation within a system of party and regional lists; the electorate would

TOGETHER, MANDELA AND DE KLERK HAD PILOTED THE **SHIP OF STATE** TO SAFE HARBOUR

Thousands patiently wait in line in 1994 to choose their first-ever democratic government.

choose a central government and nine regional governments. In September Nelson Mandela had called for the lifting of all remaining international sanctions. Two months later he and De Klerk shared the 1993 Nobel Peace Prize: the two stood on opposite sides of the racial divide, but they held each other in respect, f not affection, and together they had piloted the ship of state to safe harbour.

The last of the obstacles to settlement quickly and, it seemed, miraculously evaporated. A few days prior to the election, in a startling turn-around, Buthelezi finally abandoned his demands for postponement and greater autonomy for the provinces, and agreed to participate in the polls.

After a protracted election process, which proved a lively, often chaotic but always – astonishingly in view of past antagonisms – good-humoured affair, the ANC gained a near-two-thirds majority in the new National Assembly. It also captured healthy majorities in six of the nine regional parliaments, shared the honours in the seventh, lost the Western Cape to the National Party (the conservative coloured vote proved decisive) and KwaZulu-Natal to the Inkatha Freedom Party. The Pan-Africanist Congress was virtually annihilated at the polls.

Early in May 1994, Nelson Mandela was sworn in as the first president of a liberated, fully democratic South Africa.

THE NEW FREEDOM

The years since the transfer of power in 1994 have been ones of steady transition – political, social, economic – though the road has been rough in patches, bedevilled by the occasional U-turn and blind alley and by the inability of the new order, despite the best of intentions, to deliver the fruits of freedom to its constituents. Nevertheless the country has taken enormous strides: democracy is firmly established; the constitution is the envy of the world, its Bill of Rights a technically faultless guardian of civil liberties; black empowerment is making headway in the workplace; South Africa is ranked among the most progressive of Africa's nations and, indeed, is seen as the key to the future of what has been perceived by some as 'the hopeless continent'.

In the realm of governance, perhaps the most significant development in the years following the political revolution has been the shift away from old-style socialism. The African National Congress came to power as a liberation movement which subscribed to, was inspired by, the principles enshrined in the Freedom Charter (see page 46) but the realities of globalization, the information revolution and the New Economy prompted an ideological sea change. South Africa is a capitalist country. Although the redistribution of wealth remains the priority, it is through economic growth and the free play of market forces that society is to be nurtured and the poor uplifted.

South Africa has also, to a degree, been formally purged of its past. In April 1996 the Truth and Reconciliation Commission, a mobile body chaired by Nobel laureate Desmond Tutu, was convened to expose (and, when requested, to forgive) 'political' crimes committed during the apartheid era. Its mission was founded on the biblical axiom that 'the truth shall set you free', and during the next few years, as the worms crawled out of the woodwork in their dozens, it did manage to exorcise some of the ghosts. Its hearings were seen to be fair, and highly valuable to the process of national reconciliation.

To Mandela, indeed, the campaign for reconciliation became something close to a crusade. It was his passionate advocacy of racial harmony that enabled the new country to hold together in its most difficult, most uncertain years, and to emerge as an object lesson in sensitive accommodation.

He was also a hard act to follow. Nelson Mandela, father of post-apartheid South Africa and among the century's most respected statesmen, relinquished the burden of presidential office to his protégé Thabo Mbeki in 1999. The 'miracle' of peaceful transition was over; the government now had to tackle the unglamorous, controversial, essential business of nuts-and-bolts transformation at all levels. The enemies were formidable, among them pressures to create First-World social services in a developing country with massive poverty and unemployment, a critical shortage of expertise in the delivery areas of the public service, creaking educational and health systems that stubbornly refused to respond to the thrust of new policies, a threatened crisis of expectation, a labour movement holding to the proletarian principles of the past, the ravages of AIDS, residual racism on the one hand and the psychology of 'entitlement' on the other, crime and corruption.

Nevertheless, there has been a lot of progress; the issues are being vigorously debated, and confronted; good leaders are at the helm in key areas of endeavour, and the future is full of hope. South Africans have proved to the world that they can work their way through what has seemed the most intractable of difficulties. Above all they have learned the meaning, and the value, of freedom.

Nobel laureate Desmond Tutu seeks truth and reconciliation.

SOUTH AFRICA has seen rapid and fundamental change. Within the space of a few years a hazardous and sometimes painful transition from autocratic white minority rule to full democracy has taken place. Its political and, to a lesser degree, its economic institutions have been restructured, its society transformed.

GOVERNMENT

Principal ingredients of the constitution are an executive president, a National Assembly, nine provincial parliaments (technically, legislative assemblies), a Council of Provinces with limited powers, and a Bill of Rights. To elaborate:

• The constitution is the supreme law. Statutes enacted by parliament must be in accordance with the constitution, some of whose clauses restrict parliamentary discretion, for instance, in matters affecting the Bill of Rights and the powers of the provinces.

• The National Assembly comprises 400 members elected through a system of proportional representation: the number of seats held by each party is calculated according to the total (countrywide) votes it receives in a general election. Of the 400 members, 200 are elected on a national list and 200 on provincial lists.

• The president is the head of state and is elected by the National Assembly from among its members. He appoints the deputy president and cabinet ministers, assigns them their functions, and may dismiss them.

• In a radical departure from the Westminster tradition, the system makes no provision for members of the National Assembly to represent specific constituencies (though they may be, and have been, allocated to such constituencies by their party leaders). Nor, in practice, can members vote independently in parliament: they belong to their political grouping, so the members are more or less forced to adhere strictly to the party line. These two elements are perceived by some as major flaws in the structure of representative government in South Africa.

• Regional government: each of the nine provinces has its own legislature, or parliament, of between 30 and 100 members (the exact number depends on population size) and an executive council (cabinet) comprising the provincial premier and 10 ministers. The legislature may change the provincial constitution provided that two-thirds of its members are in agreement and that it does not conflict with the national constitution.

The powers of a provincial parliament are not cast in stone: there must be proven administrative capacity, and authority is conferred by the central government. Among its functional areas are agriculture, cultural affairs, schooling (but not university education), health,

Art in the streets of Johannesburg (*opposite*). The Newtown urban renewal scheme promises to transform the city's decaying central area. *Above, from left to right*: Cape Town's cobbled and tree-shaded Greenmarket Square; local soccer fans and their idols; and the new heart of Johannesburg, Sandton.

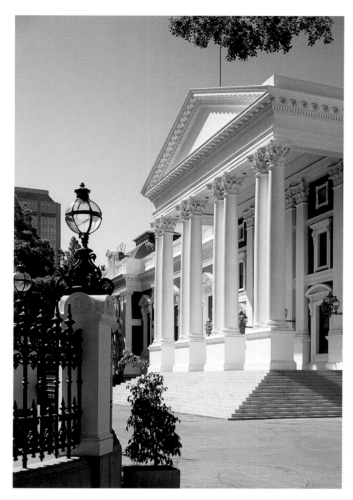

Cape Town's elegant parliament building backs onto the Company Gardens, which began life more than three centuries ago. Cape Town is South Africa's legislative capital.

housing, welfare, local government, police services, the environment, conservation, tourism, sport and recreation, gambling, roads, transport, airports, traditional authorities and customary law, and regional planning and development.

• The constitution also recognizes the status and role of traditional leadership and customary law in South Africa. This recognition is given substance in the deliberations of the national and the six provincial houses of traditional leaders.

• Local government is perceived as the engine of upliftment and growth; local authorities are being restructured; more and more powers are being devolved to local level. There are three categories of local authority, the most advanced embracing the larger metropolitan areas, or 'unicities' – greater Johannesburg, Pretoria, East Rand, Durban, Cape Town and greater Port Elizabeth – which will in due course become 'states within states' handling huge budgets and taking on more and more of the responsibilities that were traditionally fulfilled by the central government. If the vision is realized and global trends are sustained, these unicities will become large and self-sufficient enough to compete, as integrated units, in the international marketplace.

• A Charter of Fundamental Rights (bill of rights) safeguards the ordinary citizen from unjust action by the State and, in certain cases, by other individuals. In doing so, it also protects the rights of communities and cultural groups. Every person has the right to, among other things, life; equality in law; freedom from discrimination, security (detention without trial is specifically prohibited); freedom to own property; freedom of conscience, opinion, religion, language, custom, association, speech and peaceful protest; the right to basic education, to a healthy environment, to fair labour practices, and to a secret vote.

• The Constitutional Court is the final authority on all matters relating to the interpretation, protection and enforcement of the constitution. The court sits in Johannesburg.

FOREIGN POLICY

South Africa is a minor player on the world stage. But, in Africa, the Republic has pre-eminent standing and a crucial role to fulfil. It enjoys the status of a regional super-power. It covers just 3 per cent of the continent's surface and is home to a bare 5 per cent of its population, yet it accounts for four-tenths of Africa's industrial output; two-thirds of electricity generated; about half of Africa's mineral production; 40 per cent (in normal years) of maize production; and two-thirds of steel production. South Africans drive nearly half of Africa's motor vehicles, use more than a third of its telephones and are way ahead of other African countries in the Internet stakes.

The smaller states within the southern subcontinent rely heavily on and co-operate closely with South Africa. The rand monetary area encompasses Namibia and the independent kingdoms of Swaziland and Lesotho; the customs union includes the aforementioned plus Botswana. The economies of Zimbabwe and Zambia are largely dependent on South Africa's communications network and its seaports.

With globalization and the rearrangement of the world into trading blocs, collective enterprises such as the Southern African Development Community (SADC) are vital to regional prosperity – and the impetus within them can come only from South Africa. Nor are such enterprises confined to the economic sphere: already there are structures in place for collective conflict-resolution (the 'invasion' of Lesotho in the late 1990s was the resolution in action), and there is talk of a southern African bill of rights.

Co-operation extends much farther afield. Even during the sanctions era, when contact with the apartheid regime was a cloak-and-dagger affair of covert communication and clandestine agreements, cross-border rail deals were netting South Africa R800 million a year – an impressive enough figure, but modest in relation to what has since been and will in future be negotiated. In 1994, the first year of the new era, Kenya signed a R40-million lease contract for locomotives and, according to reports, South Africa's Transnet utility had agreed to survey Sudan's rail system, as well as to supply that country with a fleet of 100 giant tankers to ferry in essential crude-oil imports. Large-scale Transnet projects had also been completed or were in progress in Angola, Mozambique and Malawi, and new ones were being discussed with authorities in the then Zaïre (now Democratic Republic of Congo), the Republic of Congo, Tanzania and Ivory Coast.

Similarly, South Africa's Eskom envisages harnessing the southern region's immense hydro-electric power potential to provide, through an international grid, cheap electricity to countries as far north as the equator. Eventually the scheme could link the generating resources of the Kunene and Congo rivers in the west with lakes Victoria and Malawi and the Zambezi River (already straddled by the giant Cahora Bassa dam) in the centre and east.

The regions of Africa have shared interests and they are drawing closer together – under southern leadership. All this has its wider implications. In Europe and America, South Africa is seen as the best hope for a continent ravaged by poverty, disease, famine and civil upheaval. The industrial world has poured billions of dollars into various forms of disaster relief – unrecoverable funds that could have been far better spent on economic development, long-term health care and the provision of badly needed infrastructure.

United States policy towards Africa, unstructured and even opportunistic in the past, now seems to be taking on a definite shape, best described perhaps by the phrase 'preventive diplomacy'. A great deal more could have been done, so the thinking goes, to pre-empt the indescribable horrors of Rwanda, civil war in Angola, Burundi, the Democratic Republic of Congo, Sierra Leone and elsewhere, disintegration in Somalia, famine in Ethiopia, had more analytical forethought been devoted to the ominous trends, and the crises nipped in the bud.

Preventive diplomacy involves more than stockpiling food and blankets against the evil day. It calls for a partnership between the United States, together with the other G7 nations, and an enlightened, comparatively powerful regional leadership. South Africa is well placed to assume the part – and has already assumed it.

The task is formidable. President Mbeki's much-debated vision of an 'African Renaissance' has been tarnished by constant conflict on a continent where regional groups compete for power and for its resources (notably oil and diamonds) and where, all too often, the government's writ barely extends beyond the grounds of the presidential palace. Nor does old-fashioned loyalty to fellow leaders of the continental liberation struggle help Mbeki's cause: his initial failure, in 2000, to condemn the abuses of human and property rights in neighbouring Zimbabwe, or at least distance his government's policies from them, fuelled global perceptions that the entire region was vulnerable, which affected the flow of vital foreign investment to South Africa.

On the wider front, South Africa is in the vanguard of a campaign, one that is rapidly gaining momentum, to narrow the wealth gap between the 'rich north' and the 'poor south', to lower trade barriers, to distribute the fruits of the electronically driven New Economy more evenly, and to restructure global institutions – including the United Nations (UN), the World Bank and the International Monetary Fund (IMF).

DEFENCE

Despite international sanctions imposed during the apartheid era (see page 48) – or rather, largely because of them – South Africa managed to maintain a well-equipped, powerful defence force, one of the biggest and certainly the most formidable in Africa. Local weapons and equipment manufacture, co-ordinated by the government-owned Armscor organization, filled most of the gaps created by mandatory military embargoes. The degree of technical sophistication, achieved in a relatively short time, was impressive by any standards. From South African production lines came a large range of military vehicles designed to suit local conditions; new weapons systems (including the high-precision G5 155-mm field gun and its mobile version, the G6); tanks (the Olifant); over 200 different types of ammunition; communications systems (the advanced frequency-tapping two-way radio); Impala and Cheetah (adapted Mirage 111s) jet aircraft; and a combat helicopter.

The post-apartheid South African National Defence Force (SANDF) is manned by a core of experienced regulars, whose principal preoccupation since 1994 has been the integration of a motley array of military bodies – the permanent force of the old regime, the armies of the four formerly 'independent' homelands, and the armed wings of the liberation organizations. Senior officers have been promoted from the higher echelons of all these units.

A multi-billion dollar deal with British, Swedish, German and French interests to upgrade air and naval hardware was concluded in 1999; reciprocal investments would, said the government, more than make up for the cost of the purchases. Many South Africans, however, question the wisdom of spending billions on a capability more suited to the old Cold War days. External aggression remains the remotest of threats; what the country really needs are more troops on the ground – mobile infantry trained to help the police maintain internal order and to put out the occasional regional fire.

The 130,000-strong police force, like the army, has undergone fundamental change. Until 1994 it was widely regarded as the coercive arm of a repressive regime, and enjoyed neither the confidence nor the respect of the majority. It is being restructured and retrained to be apolitical, flexible,

Simon's Town in False Bay is the southernmost of the Cape Peninsula's centres, and is the headquarters of the South African navy.

to serve rather than to intimidate – and to catch criminals. A high crime rate, typical perhaps of societies in transition and particularly those afflicted with massive poverty and unemployment, has challenged its competence. The formation of the elite Scorpions unit, of a detective training school and of an assets seizure unit (which confiscates ill-gotten gains) are some of many steps taken to turn the tide.

JUSTICE

The first settlers at the Cape brought the laws of Holland with them: a code evolved from the Germanic laws of western Europe, many of which in turn originated in the *Corpus Juris Civilis*, the four great books prescribed by the Eastern Roman (Byzantine) Emperor Justinian in the sixth century. Despite the systematic anglicization of the Cape from the early nineteenth century onwards, a royal commission found, in 1857, that 'the Roman-Dutch law forms the great bulk of the law in the Colony'. Nevertheless, British influence on the legal system has been considerable, particularly in the realms of court procedure, common law precedent, company and mercantile jurisprudence, and in the rules of evidence.

The British system of judgment by peers – trial by jury – was established by the first Charter of Justice in 1827. However, it never proved effective (white juries rarely convicted white defendants in cases where race played a part) and was progressively abandoned after the Act of Union in 1909. In 1969, it was formally and completely abolished in favour of a more workable alternative procedure: a single judge or, in serious cases, a judge with two assessors.

During the period from Union in 1910 to liberation in 1994, a huge and complex network of control legislation overlay common law, but the apartheid statutes have now disappeared, to be replaced by a profusion of enlightened measures. Among the more notable of the latter are those outlawing discrimination in all its forms and seeking to guarantee transparency and freedom of information.

Ultimate authority in constitutional matters is vested in the Constitutional Court. There is also a Public Protector, nominated by a joint committee of both houses of parliament (the appointment must be approved by a 75 per cent majority), who protects the ordinary citizen from 'administrative misbehaviour'.

In non-constitutional matters, parliament remains supreme. For the rest, the legal structure comprises the Court of Appeal, which sits in Bloemfontein (the country's judicial capital), highest of the working courts and composed of the Chief Justice together with as many appeal judges as the state president may determine; the provincial and local divisions of the High Court, each presided over by a state-appointed judge who may be dismissed only by special parliamentary sanction; itinerant circuit courts (also high courts); and Magistrates' Courts (of which there are about 450), which handle the great bulk of routine and minor litigation. Many of the more complex and serious cases are heard in the Regional Magistrates' Courts. There are also separate Children's Courts, Maintenance Courts, Small Claims Courts, and less formal special courts which give judgment in disputes according to indigenous custom. These are presided over by a chief or headman; appeals against decisions may be made to a magistrate.

Less than 3 per cent of persons accused of criminal wrong had, until the mid-1990s, been represented in court, largely because of the sheer volume of 'routine' cases – those involving, for instance, identity documents (it is estimated that some 18 million people were arrested for pass law offences between 1916 and 1985). However, even with the demise of apartheid and the extension of legal aid, litigation – and representation in less serious cases – remains beyond the means of the great majority of the country's citizens. Moreover, political transition, dislocation, a shortage of administrative skills and burdensome court rolls have posed severe threats to the criminal justice and correctional services systems. The judicial process, in practice, is generally slow, cumbersome, costly and, in many respects, ill suited to the new South Africa. There is a real awareness, both within and outside the legal profession, that some basic and far-reaching changes are needed.

THE ECONOMY

South Africa is an uncomfortable mix of First-World sophistication and Third-World underdevelopment. It has immense natural resources, employs advanced technologies and supports complex industrial, commercial and financial structures. On the downside, however, education standards are generally low; there is a serious skills shortage at the top end of the jobs market; and unemployment hovers around the 40 per cent mark.

The ANC leadership is committed to the eradication of poverty through its Growth, Employment and Redistribution (GEAR) policy, a market-friendly approach which has opened the economy to foreign competition, and enabled the government to remove some exchange control restrictions, lower tariff barriers, stabilize national finances during a period of political transition and global turbulence (the emerging economies have been especially hard hit) and – a splendid achievement – to control inflation.

The challenge now is to strike the right balance. On the one hand there is an immediate and desperate need to create unskilled jobs (fully 80 per cent of the economically active population is semi-skilled, unskilled or unemployed); on the other, the country has to attract foreign investment and compete in the global environment, which means, among other things, that its workforce must become more productive, smarter, leaner. The second imperative frustrates the first, certainly in the short term, and there were massive job losses across the board in the later 1990s. The promise is that, after this period of sacrifice, a dynamic economy, capable of absorbing many more job-seekers, will emerge.

All the ingredients of dynamism, in fact, are in place. The fundamentals are sound; inflation is under control; foreign reserves and the trade balance are healthy; Gear seems to have succeeded (revised figures in 2000 indicate that the gross domestic product grew by 23 per cent, or an annual average 5.3 per cent, between 1995 and 1999, which exceeded the four-year growth target by an astonishing 44 per cent); government's stated intentions are to encourage domestic savings and foreign capital investment, privatize state assets, forge public-private partnerships, create a network of well-serviced high-growth areas (called spatial development initiatives, or SDIs – the Maputo Corridor is one such) and industrial development zones (IDZs – for example, the Eastern

Cape's Coega deep-water harbour and steel-making complex), and guide what is still, in many respects, a smoke-stack economy into the electronic age. A key, though long-term, objective of the overall strategy is the economic integration of the sub-continent, largely through the agency of the Southern African Development Community (SADC).

The most vital element of success, for both South Africa and the wider region, is foreign direct investment (FDI). Africa as a whole continues to languish on the fringes of the international economy, attracting a miserly 1.2 per cent of global FDI; South Africa itself, which, together with Egypt, Angola, Nigeria and Morocco, enjoys the bulk of the modest investment flow, received just $1.4 billion in 1999, despite numerous favourable economic statistics and a high investment grade from Standard and Poor, the international rating agency.

What foreign investment there is tends to be privatization driven, and, as mentioned, this is an option the government has chosen despite opposition from the unions and the political left. South Africa has a top-heavy public sector and an asset sale could release billions for the fight against poverty. More sustainable would be the impetus – to productivity, to economic growth and (in time) to job creation – prompted by sales to or, more usually, by working partnerships with the private sector, at both national and local level.

The most significant contributions to the gross domestic product are the manufacturing industry (about 23 per cent), financial services (20 per cent), energy (15 per cent), the informal sector (estimated 10 per cent), transport and communications (10 per cent), and mining (6.4 per cent). Agriculture, forestry and fishing account for a relatively modest 4 per cent. These figures reveal the dramatic transformation from an agrarian-based economy just over a century ago, before the discovery and exploitation of diamonds and gold, to fairly advanced industrialization.

For much of the twentieth century mining provided the dynamic. After the Second World War there was an impressive growth in manufacturing activity, but the emphases are again changing, rapidly and fundamentally: technology, information and e-commerce are the new engines of growth, and South Africa is struggling to remain on the right side of the great digital divide that is separating the rich nations of the world from the poor ones, and which threatens to overwhelm the latter. The country is ahead of the rest of the continent in the race for global connection, but that is not saying a great deal: currently, Africans account for less than one per cent of the world's Internet users. Moreover, if present trends continue, the South African IT industry will be more than 60 per cent short of the technicians it needs by the year 2003 – not counting higher-grade computer experts and programmers.

Clearly, the country needs to halt the 'brain drain' that is inhibiting economic growth, to import foreign expertise in the short term, and to produce and keep its own technological experts in the long one.

MINING South Africa has the largest known reserves of gold, platinum, high-grade chromium, manganese, vanadium, fluorspar and andalusite in the world, and massive deposits of diamonds, iron-ore, coal, uranium, asbestos, nickel and phosphates – a power-ful litany of natural endowment. The country's gold mines are the

The gold-mining industry, once the bedrock of the country's economy, plays a diminishing – but still very significant – role in the process of wealth creation.

third largest of the world's suppliers of uranium, a co-product. Gold, however, has taken a beating in recent years: international crises – the kind that have traditionally attracted support for the metal – have failed to lift the price above what, for many of South Africa's mines, is a break-even level.

Diamonds, discovered in the deep kimberlite pipes of what is now the Northern Cape, launched the country's industrial revolution in the 1870s and generated fabulous wealth over the decades that followed. The country is the world's largest producer of gem diamonds.

Among the most important of the minerals is manganese, vital in the production of steel and found in great quantities (about 80 per cent of the world's known reserves) in the Northern Cape. About three-quarters of the earth's reserves of both chromium and platinum-group metals (palladium, rhodium, iridium and ruthenium as well as platinum itself) are locked into the immense pre-Cambrian strata of South Africa's bushveld complex in the northern part of the country.

Finally there is coal, of which South Africa has located deposits amounting to 58 billion tons, and which provides the country with much of its electricity and synthetic fuels. The 100 or so collieries in the country produce about 200 million tons a year; a healthy proportion of the output is exported, most of it through the east coast port of Richards Bay and mainly to northern Europe and Japan.

Koeberg, near Cape Town, is the country's only nuclear plant; other, smaller ones are planned.

ENERGY Despite its limited oil resources, South Africa is a net exporter of energy, and ranks as one of the world's four cheapest producers of electricity. Coal, as mentioned, is the principal source: 60 per cent of coal-mining output is applied to the generation of electricity; 17 per cent to the production of synthetic fuels; six per cent to conversion to coke and tar. Three great oil-from-coal plants have been built: Sasol 1 in the Free State, completed in 1955; and Sasol 2 and 3 at Secunda in Mpumalanga, the impetus for the latter two coming from the international oil crisis in 1973. Together, these establishments represent the world's first and as yet only commercial (albeit subsidized) large-scale synthetic fuel operation, which supplies just over 35 per cent of domestic consumption. Fuel prices are generally lower than those in western Europe.

South Africa's largest utility, Eskom, which operates coal-fired, hydro-electric, gas-turbine plants and a nuclear power station, provides 97 per cent of electricity consumed domestically. It also exports profitably to neighbouring countries: Mozambique, Botswana and Zimbabwe are reliant on South African electricity. Indeed, as we've seen, Eskom generates around 60 per cent of all power produced on the continent of Africa, and could comfortably supply enough electricity for the needs of every country south of the Sahara. The utility's annual turnover is bigger than the gross domestic products of most African states.

Offshore oil and gas fields have been located off the south coast town of Mossel Bay, and the first exploitation contracts were awarded in the early 1990s. Currently, Mossgas, the operating company, produces about 30,000 barrels of oil a day, and brings ashore some 1.5 million tons of natural gas and 250,000 tons of condensate a year. Indications of the presence of even larger gas fields off the country's western seaboard emerged towards the end of 2000.

Solar power generation is in its infancy but the possibilities are enormous, especially in the remoter rural areas for lighting and heating schools, clinics and houses, and to replace wood and charcoal (which are precious environmental resources on the one hand and dangerous pollutants on the other) with electricity. ESKOM has launched an ambitious research programme (based on US renewable power technology) which, if early promise is fulfilled, will prove to the world that solar energy can be harnessed to generate electricity in quantity and at costs that will compete with coal and gas. The utility is well on the way to establishing that the sun's heat can be stored, in a solar thermal plant, for distribution not only during daylight hours but at night as well. Plans, reported in South Africa's *Financial Mail*, are well advanced for the construction of a giant demonstration solar 'larder' near Upington in the sunny Karoo. The plant will cost up to R1 billion and supply 100 megawatts of power at about the same price as coal-fired electricity – that is, at just 10 per cent of the cost international experts have hitherto considered attainable.

Dramatic advances on the nuclear front are also on the horizon. Centrepiece of Eskom's blueprint is the innovative Pebble Bed Nuclear Reactor (PBMR), a small (and relatively cheap) installation which is said to be ultra-safe, clean and capable of generating power at about 16 cents a kilowatt-hour. The existing Koeberg plant near Cape Town has been earmarked as the preferred site for the building of a demonstration module. If the project is successful, it will lead to more domestic nuclear installations, to foreign sales of at least 20 such plants a year, and to the creation of more than 90,000 jobs. The PBMR company's chief executive officer told the *Mail*: 'If we meet our targets, we will change the world; if we don't, we'll change our jobs.' He and his team are, however, confident of a stunning breakthrough in energy production.

INDUSTRY A large pool of labour, a wealth of natural resources, technological expertise and, not least, economic and perhaps political necessity during the apartheid era have led South Africa towards self-sufficiency in most products. Manufacturing industry accounts for almost a quarter of the gross domestic product. With the lowering of trade tariffs, however, many local enterprises are facing stiff competition from imports, and are seeking to penetrate external markets (usually with difficulty, but often with surprising success). Among the larger sub-sectors are:
• **Metals and minerals** The Iron and Steel Corporation (Iscor) produces liquid steel for both local consumption and export. A sophisticated new steel plant was constructed at Saldanha Bay, on the west coast in the 1990s; another has been earmarked for the planned Coega deep-water harbour near Port Elizabeth. Smaller mills turn out a wide range of metal products, including carbon and stainless steel, ferro alloys, copper and brass, and high-carbon chrome; engineering and heavy industrial works manufacture everything from cranes and sugar mills through engines, turbines, machine tools, agricultural equipment, structural steel and cables to specialized industrial machinery and computer products. Non-metallic mineral products (mainly for the construction industry) add billions more to the value of industrial output.
• **Transport and equipment** There are a number of vehicle manufacturing and assembly plants in the country, most in and around Port Elizabeth, the 'Detroit of South Africa'; the giant Volkswagen works

is located just inland from there in the small town of Uitenhage. In 2000 Daimler/Chrysler opened a R1.4 billion plant, in the small river-port of East London farther up the coast, that will turn out 40,000 right-hand drive C-class Mercedes a year for delivery overseas. Other large-scale export contracts have been negotiated, even though the industry seems to be especially vulnerable to labour problems. Heavy-duty diesel engines for buses are manufactured near Cape Town, gearboxes in Boksburg near Johannesburg. Railway rolling stock is also locally manufactured.

Minibus taxis have almost, but not quite, supplanted more traditional ways of getting around. The taxi industry is an important segment of the informal economy.

• **Clothing and textiles** The industry is labour-intensive, employing about 5 per cent of the total workforce, and was until recently earmarked as one of the growth points. However, the trade barriers are falling and there is fierce competition from cheap imports, both legitimate and of the 'grey' (smuggled) kind, mainly from Asia.

• **Pharmacueticals and chemicals** The list of basic industrial chemicals produced in South Africa is long, ranging across the entire spectrum from fertilizers and pesticides through explosives to petroleum products, plastics and paints.

• **Food products and wine** Again, practically the entire range is locally processed. Drought seriously affected food production in the 1990s, but exports – notably of cereals and processed foods to Africa and frozen and canned fruits to Europe – have since picked up. South African wines became a fashionable item in Europe for a while after the country rejoined the world in the early 1990s, but they are now finding it difficult to maintain the momentum in the highly competitive market.

The manufacturing sector is capable of much further expansion: South Africa exports too many raw materials that could be fabricated, turned into semi-manufactured or end products – thus absorbing a great many more job-seekers.

TRANSPORT AND COMMUNICATIONS South Africa's infrastructure is the continent's most developed; many of the countries of the subcontinent, as mentioned, depend heavily on the Republic's road and rail network.

Some 200,000 kilometres of roads interlace the country, 50,000 kilometres of which have been surfaced, together with a further 50,000 kilometres of roadworks within the urban areas. The 7,000 kilometres of the national highway network will eventually be extended to 20,000 kilometres, the programme largely financed by toll roads. The routes are used by around 6 million vehicles – but not, relatively speaking, very safely: the road death toll is one of the highest in the world.

The railways – 36,000 kilometres of track, of which 20,000 kilometres are electrified – are operated by Spoornet, a division of

the parastatal Transnet, the largest commercial enterprise in the country. Transnet features in the privatization plans; its other divisions run the national airline South African Airways (SAA), the road transport services, the harbours and the pipelines. Suburban rail networks service the Pretoria-Witwatersrand, the Durban-Pinetown and the Cape Peninsula areas. There are plans to introduce high-speed (200 kilometre per hour) inter-city trains.

SAA operates a fleet of Boeing 747 and Airbus airliners over a network that spans most of the globe. Many other international carriers offer scheduled flights to and from South Africa. Pretoria-Johannesburg, Cape Town and Durban have international airports. Comprehensive domestic air services, provided by SAA and a number of private airlines, link 50 or so centres within the country.

AGRICULTURE South Africa is one of only half a dozen or so of the world's net food-exporting countries – a testament in a sense to the expertise of its farming community and water engineers because the subcontinent's natural resources, in this sphere, are poor. Rainfall is mostly seasonal and invariably – certainly in recent years – unpredictable. The soil is not especially fertile: erosion over the millennia and the leaching of Africa's earth during the wetter periods of the continent's history have impoverished the nutrient content over large areas (only 12 per cent of the surface area is arable).

Despite these built-in drawbacks, the diversity of the country's climatic conditions (*see* page 12) enables its farmers to grow a wide variety of crops, from the sugar and subtropical fruits of KwaZulu-Natal, the deciduous fruits of the Western Cape and the great citrus plantations of Zebediela in the north, the Sundays River valley in the south and around Citrusdal in the west, through the huge maize yields of the summer-rainfall areas to the tobacco of the more arid regions; and to rear livestock for beef, pork, dairy

A regiment of wine bottles on parade in one of the Western Cape's myriad cellars. The productive winelands region sustains some 5,000 grape-growers.

products, mutton and wool. A succession of droughts and escalating input costs, and outbreaks of foot-and-mouth disease in the latter part of 2000, have, however, placed large sections of the commercial farming community under severe financial strain. The situation in the less developed and generally less well-endowed 'black' rural areas tends to deteriorate more rapidly under adverse conditions and in places has reached critical proportions.

Land is central to the post-apartheid redistribution issue. For decades parliamentary law reserved more than 80 per cent of the country for 'white' occupation, and pressure to reallocate this prized resource is intensifying. Direct expropriation without adequate compensation has been ruled out, but the white farmer is no longer coddled by the state. Over-generous assistance through the Land Bank and the Agricultural Credit Board is a thing of the past: both have been redirected towards the development sector.

The ANC government's agricultural policy is aimed at 'improving support for the neglected small-scale farming sector, promoting household food security rather than national food self-sufficiency, boosting rural employment and ending inequality in South Africa'.

TOURISM Potentially, this segment of the economy is capable of creating more jobs (and of earning foreign currency more quickly and in massive amounts) than any other single sector. South Africa, with its broad horizons, its magnificent and varied landscapes, its equable climate, its wildlife, its beautiful coastlines, its diverse human geography, the remarkably favourable exchange rate and value-for-money it offers visitors, should rank as one of the world's prime holiday and eco-tourism

destinations. That it does not, yet, can be blamed on various factors, among them 'Afro-pessimism', a high crime rate, self-defeating xenophobic attitudes, untrained and often grudging service in hotels, shops and other tourist-intensive venues, poor marketing strategies and organization, a hesitant approach to crucial public-private partnerships, and a kind of complacency founded on global admiration, now faded, for the 'miracle' of transition. The stakeholders, however – central government, the provinces and the hospitality industry – seem at last to be getting their act together. The incentive to do so is certainly powerful enough: with every eight tourists who arrive, one more South African finds a job.

According to international visitors, the south-western part of the Western Cape claims the country's top four tourist attractions. Cape Town's Victoria & Alfred Waterfront heads the list, followed by Cape Point, Table Mountain and the wine routes of the hinterland. Other prime drawcards, in descending order, are the Garden Route of the southern coast, Cape Town's Kirstenbosch botanical gardens, and the ostrich farms of the Little Karoo, the Kruger National Park, Durban's Golden Mile beachfront (the latter two a surprisingly low eighth and ninth), the Little Karoo's Cango Caves complex, Robben Island, Pretoria city, the Blyde River Canyon in Mpumalanga, Johannesburg's Gold Reef City and the resort areas of the KwaZulu-Natal Drakensberg.

LABOUR Organized labour is a powerful force for change, both in the workplace and in the political arena. The Congress of South African Trade Unions (Cosatu), the umbrella federation, is firmly linked with the African National Congress and the South African Communist Party within a formally constituted tripartite alliance. Cosatu threw its weight behind the ANC's successful election drives in the 1990s (and expected a dividend); senior Cosatu leaders have changed hats to serve in top political positions; new labour laws have appeared on the statute books.

Foremost among the latter are the Labour Relations Act, which regulates and centralizes the collective bargaining process; the Basic Conditions of Employment Act, which guarantees, among much else, minimum hours of work and overtime rates; the Skills Development Act (training); and the Employment Equity Act of 1999 (gender equality, affirmative action and so on).

In absolute terms these are highly progressive measures, but to many employers (and potential investors) they bear little relation to the real, fiercely competitive world. They burden companies with administrative expenses and load the cost of labour which, because that cost is not linked to productivity, leads to more emphasis on capital intensive investment and curtailed job opportunities at the lower end of the skills scale. South Africa already suffers massive unemployment; less than one in 10 school-leavers is able to find work, a situation that is having serious repercussions throughout the socio-economic spectrum, and given a free hand the government would probably settle for a much more flexible labour market.

Moreover, what loopholes can be found in the legislation are, naturally, being exploited by the private sector; many employers are cutting overheads by taking on casual labour and by 'outsourcing' – a euphemism in many instances for hiring a non-unionized, low-wage, low-skilled workforce. This does nothing for upliftment, and it antagonizes the unions which, because of privatization and the universal shift towards both non-manual work and self-employment, are already suffering a decline in membership.

Unsurprisingly, the marriage of convenience between organized labour and the ruling party has at times degenerated into a power struggle over the country's economic direction. The ANC, once a broad-based liberation movement wedded to socialist principles and dependent on union support, now has to satisfy a much wider range of interests – including those of employers – in order to create new jobs, attract investment, pay for its development programmes and integrate the country into the technology-driven global economy. At some point in the future there may well be a split in the alliance, perhaps leading to the formation of a separate workers' political party. At its 2000 congress, Cosatu resolved to form a union-based 'popular movement' to address 'the community and development concerns of the historically disadvantaged sections of the population'.

THE INFORMAL SECTOR Nearly half South Africa's economically active citizens are classed as unemployed or under-employed: the recessions of the apartheid years, the lifting of restrictions on individual enterprise and movement, massive migration to the cities and low levels of investment have created armies of urban jobless. As a consequence, the past decade has seen the evolution of a flourishing 'informal economy', a phrase that embraces a myriad micro-businesses ranging from backyard industries and one-person craft services through hawking and market trading to shebeens (township pubs) and taxis.

Apart from generating work opportunities and income, these tiny enterprises are helping develop much-needed skills and entrepreneurial expertise. No firm financial statistics are available (for sound reasons: the informal economy is barely regulated and, for the most part, untaxed), but it is reckoned that as much as 20 per cent of the country's total domestic income is derived from this sector.

HUMAN CAPITAL

Almost half a century of institutionalized apartheid bequeathed, among other depressing legacies, a grossly distorted economy and social services sector: in the mid-1990s around 45 per cent of the population existed 'below the minimum levels'; 2.3 million people were in 'urgent need of nutritional support' (a terrifying 72 children were dying of malnutrition and related conditions each day); AIDS-related diseases were beginning to take their toll; and the housing shortfall was estimated at over 1.5 million units (and growing by the month as thousands left the countryside for the towns and cities). The ANC-led government determined on upliftment on a massive scale; its Reconstruction and Development Programme (RDP) envisaged huge investments in:

• **Education** Ten years' free and compulsory schooling for every child; a pre-school reception for five-year-olds; adult literacy programmes; education for the 'lost generation' of youths who spent much of the troubled pre-liberation era on the streets; subsidized university and technical college training; heavy expenditure on new schools, equipment and textbooks.

• **Housing.** More than a million new houses within five years; the provision of running water to every household; proper sanitation for a million families; electricity to a million homes, and universal (and affordable) access to telephones. Urban hostels – vast, impersonal township warrens originally designed for migrant workers and for long a source of bitter inter-group conflict – were to be upgraded and converted for family use.

Aerial view of Cape Town's Crossroads informal settlement. Housing ranks high on the list of national priorities.

• **Health.** Free health care for children under six; large-scale investment in district health authorities, hospitals and clinics; the provision of basic nutritional requirements for all; supervised antenatal care and child delivery for all mothers.

• **Jobs and social welfare.** An extensive job creation programme; a living wage for all workers; compulsory six-months' paid maternity leave for working mothers; the equalization of pensions.

These were ambitious targets, too ambitious for the available resources to cope, and the formal RDP structure was dismantled (its assets were eventually transferred to the various departments of state), but the targets continue to provide the thrust of the government's upliftment programme. Progress has been patchy; lack of management experience and a shortage of administrative skills down the line have impeded delivery – to the point where some departments have been unable to spend more than a modest fraction of their allocated funds.

Notable successes have been chalked up in the realms of water, sanitation, electricity, communications and, to a somewhat lesser degree, housing (220,000 units must be built each year just to keep pace with additional demand). Education, though, has lagged behind: it will take years for the country to recover from the frightful impact of the old Bantu Education Act, and the first attempts at restructuring, which prompted the departure of thousands of experienced teachers, proved disastrous. Two studies found, in 2000, that South African Grade 4 pupils (9- and

10-year-olds) have the worst literacy and numeracy skills in Africa; the matriculation pass rates across the national board have been consistently dismal; many of the country's universities, even though comparatively well funded (about R6 billion is being pumped into them each year), are unable to produce successful graduates, especially in the fields of science and technology. These unpalatable facts are highly significant in the context of the New Economy: in South Africa: demand for tertiary qualifications has increased by 5,000 per cent over the past two decades, by 300 per cent for secondary qualifications, and has actually decreased for lower qualifications.

Much of the health programme is in place but, again, delivery has been faulty, and AIDS threatens to put severe if not intolerable strains on the system. It will also, of course, have far-reaching effects on the national economy: as more and more young people – including those with precious skills – fall sick, so the private sector will be burdened with higher employee-benefit and training costs; insurance rates will climb and government will have to

The show goes on at Johannesburg's innovative Market Theatre, a leading performing arts venue in the centre of Johannesburg.

devote an increasingly large slice of the tax pie to health care. It was estimated that, in 2000, nearly 20 per cent of the adult population was HIV-positive, 1,500 more South Africans were contracting the infection each day, and 5,000 infected babies were being born each month. The latter tragedy is especially controversial: government dragged its feet on the question of mother-to-child transmission. Indeed, the entire anti-AIDS campaign was for a time thrown into confusion by President Mbeki's ambivalent views on the fundamental nature of the disease. It was only officially acknowledged by the South African government in 2001 that HIV is the cause of AIDS.

The South African government is aware of these issues, and of the need to cherish its human capital. Given time, it should be able to lead the country and its people onto the high road.

ARTS AND CULTURE

Culturally, and in the realms of leisure, entertainment and sport, South Africa offers as varied and pleasing a fare as any other middle-sized country, and perhaps more so, because of its rich and vibrant cultural diversity.

THE PERFORMING ARTS The scene is lively, and much of it of international standard, though priorities have changed – conventional theatre, ballet, opera and symphonic music thrived in South Africa's major centres but subsidies have now been cut; some of the auditoriums have closed their doors, orchestras have disbanded. Still, the performing arts survive on talent and enthusiasm; among the more prominent venues are Durban's Playhouse and Cape Town's Artscape and Baxter theatre complexes; the Bloemfontein Opera House; and the Market Theatre in Johannesburg. Grahamstown, in the Eastern Cape, hosts the annual National Arts Festival, which attracts almost 100,000 visitors a day to make it the largest such event in the southern hemisphere. The lifting of the cultural boycott in 1993 opened the artistic floodgates, and offerings at the festival – theatre, music, dance and much else – are drawing increasingly from the creativity of other parts of Africa, and from the wider world.

MUSIC South Africa has produced a number of gifted instrumentalists, opera singers and ballet dancers. The country, though, finds it difficult to retain its own: universities and other learning centres turn out an unusual wealth of young talent which is often lost to the more sophisticated stages and concert halls of Europe and America.

Music of a different kind has emerged from the black community to make its mark beyond the borders of the country. The African people have ancient traditions, and a splendid talent for harmony and spontaneous song; folk music, in the country areas, still plays a powerful role in ceremony and ritual. Western culture, and especially religious conversion, has modified the forms of expression (or rather, has added new dimensions to them) but the talent remains untarnished. And, with urbanization, a new and distinct sound has evolved in the townships. Called *mbaqanga*, it stems in part from the original music of Africa, which was exported to America, refined there and returned as jazz which, in turn, has been changed and given a vibrant new character – a hybrid of many eras, many styles (the *mbube* vocal orchestra, lilting *marabi*, penny-whistle *kwela*, Dixieland, big-band, reggae, soul, rock), but with a personality very much its own.

South African jazz and *mbaqanga* greats include pianist Abdullah Ibrahim (formerly known as Dollar Brand), Hugh Masekela and Miriam Makeba, who made her first major impact in the 1960s with the song 'Wimoweh', while the most popular South African *mbube* (choral) group to date has been Ladysmith Black Mambazo, who worked with Paul Simon on his acclaimed *Graceland* album (1987). More recently the youthful sounds of kwaito have emerged from the townships – a local adaptation of house and hip-hop sounds, structured within a relentless dance beat, that thumps from minibus taxis and shebeens across the country.

The coloured people of the Western Cape also have their musical culture, borrowed in part from the American Deep South and its minstrel traditions but, again, with its own distinctive character. It has its most striking expression perhaps in the exuberant, banjo-backed *goemaliedtjies*, songs heard on street corners and at celebrations – cheerful melodies with often racy words whose origins tend to be obscure but which remain delightfully entertaining.

LITERATURE South Africa can claim few literary giants of the kind that one might expect to have emerged in a country of such beauty, complexity, conflict and tragedy. There has been no Steinbeck to give voice to the wrath of the poor; no James Baldwin to bring fiery articulation to ethnic consciousness; no Orwell, no Solzhenitzen. It could, though, be that very complexity that has inhibited the pen. Says Nadine Gordimer, a Nobel prize-winning novelist: 'Living in a society that has been as deeply and calculatedly compartmentalized as South Africa's has been under the colour bar, the writer's potential has unscalable limitations.'

Nevertheless, there have been and are South African writers of real stature: the much under-estimated Olive Schreiner; the eccentric Roy Campbell; the mystic Eugène Marais, and, of recent vintage, Alan Paton and Laurens van der Post who each, in his own way, has bared the soul of his beloved country; Nadine Gordimer, J.M. Coetzee and André Brink; playwright, poet and novelist (and painter) Zakes Mda; the poet Oswald Mtshali; the multi-talented Welcome Msomi; the brilliant Athol Fugard and his fellow playwright Gibson Kente.

Among the African people there is, too, a powerful tradition of oral literature – the key to their past and, perhaps, the door to the country's literary future. This has played its part in what is known as 'black theatre', a unique art form in which productions are conceived, written and performed by black artists largely for black audiences and which are noted for their sparkling spontaneity. Players tend to share in the creation of the work rather than follow a predetermined script; the shows are invariably an exuberant mix of words, music, song and dance, and some of them have been performed to acclaim on the stages of Europe and America. At one time much of the subject matter, especially in the more orthodox dramas, reflected (and protested) the harshness of life under apartheid, but authors are now moving away from localized, race-preoccupied introspection towards more universal themes.

BROADCASTING Radio and television services are comparatively extensive – compared, that is, with the size of the population. There are five national television channels, three run by the South African Broadcasting Corporation (SABC), the public broadcaster (two of its channels are linguistically mixed, together offering programmes in all eleven official languages); and two by independent commercial companies, one of them free-to-air and the other available to viewers on subscription. Global (satellite) services are readily accessible at fairly modest cost. The SABC remains the major radio broadcaster, with 16 stations, but the medium has been rationalized and a healthy number of community stations – 80 of them at the time of writing – have been licensed. There are also seven private commercial stations.

SPORT AND RECREATION

The country's wonderfully sunny climate and its long, often scenically beautiful seaboard favour outdoor activity generally and sport in particular. Conventional, competitive sporting standards suffered during the long years of isolation but the removal of race barriers, readmittance to the international arena and the launching of development programmes are now allowing the South African youth to realize their full potential.

SPECTATOR SPORTS The major spectator sports are soccer, rugby and cricket. Within the black community, the first is supreme, with more than 12,000 soccer clubs and around a million regular soccer players in South Africa. The national team, Bafana Bafana, were the victors of the 1996 African Cup of Nations and took part, without too much success, in the 1998 World Cup in France.

Rugby at the Newlands stadium in Cape Town.

Rugby is especially popular among Afrikaans-speaking South Africans, both white and coloured, though it also has a huge following among English speakers and, increasingly, within the black community. The national team, the Springboks, who have consistently ranked among the world's top four rugby-playing nations, defeated the New Zealand All Blacks to scoop the 1995 Rugby World Cup – their finest hour, and the last one of the amateur era. The cricket squad has also performed creditably, at times with outstanding success (especially in one-day internationals); South Africa will host the Cricket World Cup in 2003.

Olympic success has generally proved elusive, though the 1996 Atlanta Games are memorable for the two golds brought back by swimmer Penny Heyns and a gutsy one by tiny Josiah Thugwane, who emerged from obscurity (and poverty, and injury) to triumph in the marathon.

South Africa provides challenging terrain for the mountain-biker.

Sea-kayaking is among a range of water-related sports rapidly gaining popularity.

RECREATIONAL SPORTS Jogging and cycling are sociably popular recreations, and competitive road-running a prominent sport. The premier annual event is the Comrades Marathon, held in the middle of June, over the 89 kilometres (55 miles) between Durban and Pietermaritzburg. Almost as notable is Cape Town's Two Oceans Marathon.

Golf clubs, of which there are more than 400, welcome visitors; most courses are beautifully maintained; local golfers compete with honour on the international circuit; greats of the past include Bobby Locke and Gary Player; Ernie Els is currently the most successful South African competitor.

ADVENTURE SPORTS Watersports attract especially large numbers of participants, not only along the coasts but also on inland dams and rivers. Parts of the KwaZulu-Natal, Eastern and Western Cape shorelines provide quite magnificent opportunities for surfing, scuba-diving and angling; much of the country is equally ideal for adventure-type pursuits, notably canoeing, white-water rafting, orienteering, rock-climbing, mountain-biking, mountaineering and skydiving.

The National Hiking Way is a splendid network of main, supplementary and connecting routes that covers much of the country; individual trails vary from five kilometres to over 200 kilometres. Oldest and still among the most popular of the longer organized trails is the Otter, which makes its way through 41 kilometres of the lovely Tsitsikamma National Park, from Storms River to Nature's Valley in the Western Cape; en route there are hills and wooded valleys, streams, waterfalls and river estuaries, enchanting patches of natural forest, and rock pools filled by the warm blue waters of the Indian Ocean. The Otter, though, is just one of literally hundreds of trails from which the more energetic holidaymaker can choose, each with its distinctive character, its challenges, its special interest. Prime hiking areas are the mountains and valleys of the southern coastal belt, the scenically majestic Drakensberg foothills in the east, and the splendid Mpumalanga escarpment countryside to the west of the Kruger

National Park. The latter, moreover, offers its own wilderness trails, as do many of the country's other large sanctuaries.

Among less strenuous outdoor activities are birding (South Africa boasts around 900 indigenous species, an astonishing number of them endemic), and whale-watching. The waters off the entire 2,000-kilometre shoreline but especially those of the southern coasts play host to a wealth of whales and other marine mammals; most common of the former are the giant southern rights, which come close inshore to breed and calve in the winter and early summer months.

South Africa offers boundless opportunities for adventure sports, abseiling among them.

THE WILD KINGDOM

South Africa's special prides are the country's game and nature reserves, and its diverse and often spectacular landscapes. For the visitor, there is a great deal to see and do; the tourist industry is well organized; holidaymakers are able to stay in and to travel round the Republic in comfort and, at rates of exchange prevailing at the time of writing, can do so relatively cheaply; South Africa offers unrivalled opportunities for eco-tourism and 'adventure' activities. South Africa's wildlife heritage is remarkably rich: the country covers less than one-hundredth of the earth's land surface yet accommodates 5 per cent of its mammal and 8 per cent of its bird species.

Much of this marvellous diversity can be seen and enjoyed in the 300 or so protected areas set aside for conservation purposes. Best known of these is the Kruger National Park, an enormous expanse of sunlit bushveld that sprawls over the far north-eastern Lowveld region and hosts more than 140 different kinds of mammal, including the 'big five' (lion, leopard, elephant, rhino, buffalo), so sought after by the game-viewer.

The Kruger, though, is just one of many superb wilderness destinations. Along the eastern seaboard are the reserves of Zululand, a region blessed with a unique mix of ecosystems and a stunning profusion of life forms. The Eastern Cape has its Addo Elephant National Park. North-west of Johannesburg lies the Pilanesberg, location of one of Africa's most impressive game-stocking enterprises.

straddles the South Africa-Botswana border, and its sparse grasses, improbably, nurture cheetah, lion, wild dog and herds of antelope. Similar cross-border sanctuaries are being created or are planned for the northern KwaZulu-Natal region (part of what is known as the Lubombo Spatial Development Initiative), the Limpopo Valley (consolidating parts of South Africa, Botswana and Zimbabwe) and the Lowveld, the latter bringing together the Kruger, Zimbabwe's Gonarezhou and a segment of southern Mozambique. Until now, human encroachment has confined the wild animals of the veld, certainly the larger ones, within relatively small conservation areas; these expanded wildernesses are designed to reopen the ancient migratory routes, returning at least some of the game-rich land to its original, pristine condition.

Not that all is well with the country's wild regions. They are effectively protected, generally well managed but, as in so many other parts of Africa, they remain under constant threat – from poachers; from mining and industry; from domestic cattle and the spreading farmlands; from developers and corrupt local politicians; above all from the voracious appetite of the rural communities for water, grazing, firewood, medicinal plants, thatching materials and living-space. To people long deprived of their rights to good land, the existence of large tracts of fertile, protected and apparently unused countryside makes very little sense, and the temptation to encroach is often irresistible.

These are the intractable problems of Africa, indeed of the entire developing world, and they are likely to remain with us for a long time. There is, however, room for optimism, or at least hope. The decision-makers have been persuaded that the well-being of wildlife and the interests of tourism need not be in conflict with the needs of the rural people, and recent years have seen the appearance of what is variously called the 'multi-use', the 'resource' and the 'contractual' area – integrated reserves in which the people of the country-side, instead of being moved away from the conservation project (as they were, often controversially, in the past), stay where they are and help look after the environment. In return, they are able to share in its resources – and benefit financially from tourism development. It is a win-win approach: – and it holds great promise for the future.

Superb wildlife sanctuaries are among the country's biggest tourism drawcards, a number of them offering the visitor the opportunity of seeing Africa's 'big five'.

The priorities in South Africa, in short, have undergone a dramatic change, and the voice of the conservationist is heard and understood a lot more clearly than it was even a decade ago. The message is simple: humankind's assault on the environment must be controlled if the earth as we know it is to survive.

Drive westwards and you'll eventually reach the great sandy wastes of the Kalahari, first of southern Africa's transfrontier or 'peace' parks. It is called the Kgalagadi Transfrontier Park; it

JOHANNESBURG, A CITY BUILT ON **GOLD** AND NOW THE COUNTRY'S INDUSTRIAL AND **FINANCIAL HEARTLAND**

4

5

6

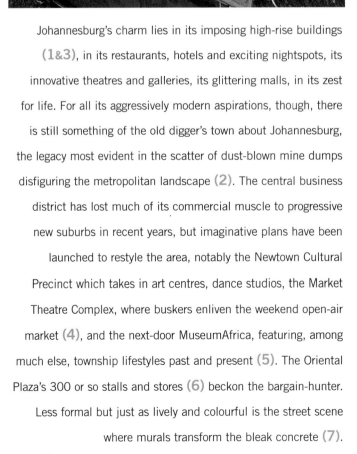

Johannesburg's charm lies in its imposing high-rise buildings (1&3), in its restaurants, hotels and exciting nightspots, its innovative theatres and galleries, its glittering malls, in its zest for life. For all its aggressively modern aspirations, though, there is still something of the old digger's town about Johannesburg, the legacy most evident in the scatter of dust-blown mine dumps disfiguring the metropolitan landscape (2). The central business district has lost much of its commercial muscle to progressive new suburbs in recent years, but imaginative plans have been launched to restyle the area, notably the Newtown Cultural Precinct which takes in art centres, dance studios, the Market Theatre Complex, where buskers enliven the weekend open-air market (4), and the next-door MuseumAfrica, featuring, among much else, township lifestyles past and present (5). The Oriental Plaza's 300 or so stalls and stores (6) beckon the bargain-hunter. Less formal but just as lively and colourful is the street scene where murals transform the bleak concrete (7).

7

For decades Johannesburg's Market Theatre (1), a 90-year-old building that once did duty as the Indian Fruit and Citrus Market – as this old advert in the theatre complex testifies (2) – has been at the cutting edge of the country's performing arts. Today the wider complex includes shops, galleries, bars, bistros and four auditoriums which, between them, cater for all tastes. Here too you'll find Kippie's jazz bar (3). The bar is named in honour of Morolong 'Kippie' Moeketsi, whose talent was nurtured in the Sophiatown of the 1940s and 1950s and who went on to play with the Shantytown Sextet and the celebrated Abdullah Ibrahim. Sellers of traditional medicine (4) enjoy steady local custom in the city. Beyond the city centre, The Bassline in Melville (5) is another notable music venue.

6

7

8

9

10

Melville (6) is a trendy Johannesburg suburb a short drive from the city centre, and known for its nightlife and restaurants (7). For African arts and crafts, the upper end of the market is catered for by outlets such as the Kim Sacks Gallery in Parkwood (8), while displays of beadwork and other crafts, like these ones in Rosebank (9) attract tourists with money to spend and, occasionally, fashionable collectors of African art. Among Johannesburg's more placid leisure venues is Zoo Lake (10).

GAUTENG

The cosmopolitan city. Johannesburg has been a magnet for immigrant folk since the first tents were erected on the newly discovered goldfields little more than a century ago. Thousands of temporary Chinese labourers were brought in to work the gold mines shortly after the Anglo-Boer War; a few chose to remain. Other Chinese families joined them, and traces of their culture are evident in the city (1) today, especially in Derrick Avenue in Cyrildene, now known as 'New Chinatown' (2).

Mohandas Gandhi, father of modern India, practised law in the young metropolis and his home (3) is preserved as a monument. This wall mosaic (4) in Troyeville is of Portuguese origin; many Portuguese from the former Portuguese territories of Mozambique and Angola having settled in Johannesburg. More recent are arrivals from the often troubled countries north of the Limpopo, many of whom have congregated in the never-sleeping inner suburbs of Yeoville and Hillbrow.

5

6

A popular leisure venue is Fisherman's Village (5) on Bruma Lake, a pleasant, man-made stretch of water. The cobbled-street village offers restaurants, coffee-houses, speciality shops, a fleamarket, a boardwalk and street entertainers (6). Even more popular are soccer matches, some of them staged in the giant Ellis Park stadium (7). Here a keen fan waits for the big game to begin (8). Early Johannesburgers, with a fine appreciation of the priorities, launched Turffontein racetrack (9) a bare year after the great gold-strike of 1886 – even before building their school and hospital. Grand new casinos compete for the lucrative gambling trade but the track, with its superb facilities, is holding its own.

7

8

9

GAUTENG

Journey into the past. Among Johannesburg's prime attractions is Gold Reef City, a 'living museum' and theme park built on the site of the historic Crown Mine. Its headgear (1) is now silent, but there's plenty of life around it. Visitors can explore the underground workings, observe gold being poured (2), watch traditional dancing displays, and enjoy fun-rides (3). Other attractions include a Victorian funfair and tea parlour and re-creations of early shops, brewery, newspaper office, stock exchange and the grand old Theatre Royal. The complex incorporates a period-style five-star hotel and casino (4).

5

6

7

8

City within a city. To the south-west of central Johannesburg lies Soweto, a vast, dense sprawl of mostly modest little houses but also of rudimentary shacks at one end of the scale and some fine residences at the other. Soweto, home to around two million people, is famed for its part in the liberation struggle – it was here, in 1976, that students rose in revolt to create the first cracks in the monstrous apartheid structure. Big business has begun to move in, but Soweto is still largely a dormitory area – commercial activity resides for the most part in a flourishing, though often troubled, taxi industry (5), in the 3,000 or so tiny 'spaza' home-based stores, and in a myriad street enterprises (6). Tours of the townships take in a restaurant (7), the Mandela House Museum (8), and the poorer residential parts (9).

9

GAUTENG

The focus of Johannesburg's business life has shifted from the central district to the northern areas, notably to Hyde Park, Sandton and Rivonia. Sandton City, Sandton Square (1&2) and Village Walk (3) are the fashionable venues. Randburg's Waterfront (4) is a large and lively leisure area of bistros and boutiques, pubs and nightspots.

5

6

7

8
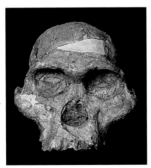

9

To the west of the city, near Krugersdorp, you'll find the old Kromdraai mine (5), which began life five years before the Witwatersrand's main reef was discovered, and the Sterkfontein cave complex (6), an archaeological treasure-house (and now a World Heritage Site) that has yielded an astonishing number of humanoid fossils over the decades, including the skull of the female human-ape known as 'Mrs Ples' (8). Also worth visiting in the area are the Krugersdorp Game Reserve (7). Beyond the immediate vicinity of the city, the Witwatersrand Botanical Garden (9) provides a home for the more restful spirits.

1

PRETORIA – THE 'JACARANDA CITY', A **JOYFUL RIOT** OF **LILAC COLOURED BLOSSOMS** IN THE SPRINGTIME

3

4

5

Pretoria, nestling in a warm and fertile river valley half an hour's drive north of Johannesburg, is the country's administrative capital, a handsome metropolis of tall buildings and stately churches (1,2&5), parks, gardens and thoroughfares graced by some 80,000 jacaranda trees (3). The city grew up around Church Square (4), which is dominated by sculptor Anton van Wouw's bronze statue of 'Oom Paul' Kruger. Buildings of note around the spacious piazza include the Old Raadsaal, or parliament; the graceful Palace of Justice, and the Reserve Bank, designed by celebrated architect Herbert Baker.

GAUTENG

Pretoria's zoo, an expanse of parkland in the heart of the city, is world renowned for its splendid array of southern African and exotic animals. Among its residents are the four great apes, the big cats and the world's most comprehensive collection of antelope. Visitors can survey the gardens (1) from the cable-car (2). Graceful flamingos (3) are part of the zoo's bird complement. Pretoria's other venues of note are Melrose House (4), where, in May 1902, Boer and Briton signed the peace treaty that ended their devastating war, and Transvaal President Paul Kruger's modest home, now a museum (5).

6

7

8

With a view over the city (6), the corridors of power
wind through Pretoria's Union Buildings (7), an
elegant crescent-shaped edifice on the heights of
Meintjes Kop. The complex was designed by Herbert
Baker and opened in 1913 in celebration of the
unification of white South Africa. Pretoria is also
proud of its museums, foremost among which is
the Museum of Natural History (8), famed for
its bird hall, its humanoid fossil displays
and its 'Life's Genesis' exhibition.

GAUTENG

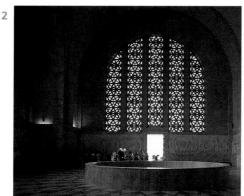

The Voortrekker Monument (1&2), an austerely massive memorial to the Great Trek of Boer families from the colonial Cape in the 1830s and 1840s, stands on Monument Hill south of central Pretoria. More modest and arguably more moving is the home (3), at nearby Irene, of Jan Smuts, soldier, statesman, philosopher and perhaps South Africa's greatest leader of the pre-democratic era.

The southern Ndebele people settled in an area north of Pretoria and some still follow the old ways. Traditional Ndebele dwellings are surrounded by walled courtyards decorated with vibrantly colourful geometical designs (4). The murals are created by the women – who are often works of art themselves (6). Their dress style incorporates beaded blankets and aprons, and metal rings around the ankles, the arms and the neck. They are also known for the colourful dolls (5) they produce. Easily reached from Pretoria and Johannesburg are a number of cultural villages showcasing traditional arts and lifestyles. The Lesedi complex (7) focuses on the Xhosa, Zulu, Bapedi and Basotho groups, their customs, costumes, crafts and homes. Other venues are devoted to the Ndebele heritage.

81

1

THE **LOST CITY,** AN OPULENTLY ORNATE AFFAIR OF DOMES,
MINARETS, AND STATUARY OF **MONUMENTAL CHARACTER**

2

3

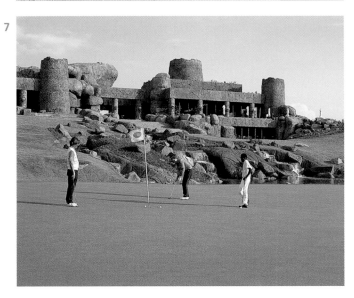

Pride of the North West is Sun City and its almost surreal Lost City neighbour, with its entrancing Palace of the Lost City Hotel (1,2,3&4), Amphitheatre (5) and the Temple of Creation (6). The hotel-casino and entertainment resort was launched by entrepreneur Sol Kerzner in the late 1970s, when gambling was forbidden in South Africa but legal in the 'independent' homeland of Bophuthatswana. The combined complex embraces four hotels, ranging from the homely Cabanas to the unashamedly luxurious Palace of the Lost City. The landscaping – both here and around Sun City – is magnificent, incorporating thousands of plants and trees (representing 22 vegetation zones), two state-of-the-art golf courses (7) and a wealth of water features, including the Valley of Waves (8). The latter boasts artificially created ocean rollers and a beach.

Among the three hotels at Sun City (4) is the Cascades (1), which offers five-star quality. Its immediate surrounds are a playground of lawns, pools, waterfalls and tropical plants.

The 620-seat Extravaganza Theatre and the casino (2) are part of the nearby Sun City Hotel.

The Entertainment Centre (3) boasts restaurants, bars, conference halls, shops and the vast, multi-purpose superbowl auditorium.

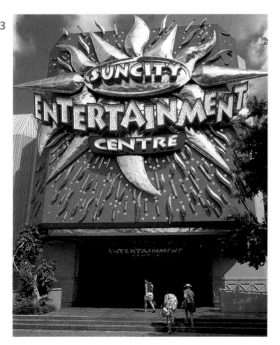

5

6

7

The Pilanesberg National Park **(5,6&7)** was created from almost nothing during the 1980s in a splendid game-stocking exercise known as 'Operation Genesis'. Animals were translocated from elsewhere in southern Africa, including rhino from KwaZulu-Natal, eland from Namibia, elephant from the Eastern Cape and zebra from Mpumalanga. The Pilanesberg's wildlife complement now includes the 'Big Five' plus giraffe, hippo and a host of antelope and other mammals. Altogether, the park is haven for more than 10,000 head of game.

To the west of Pretoria lies the Magaliesberg, a low ridge of hills that is a magnet for people who live in the concrete jungles to the east: they come to enjoy the tranquillity, the beauty of the vistas, the pleasant drives, walks and hikes (1) and the birdlife. The Magaliesberg featured briefly in the war of 1899–1902, and there are some stirring local legends of valour and endurance. Among the few visible legacies of the conflict is this British-built blockhouse (2). Recommended excursions include the Magalies Meander (3). An exhilarating alternative is a trip by hot-air balloon (4).

THE MAGALIESBERG HAS AN **AFRICAN WOODLAND** BEAUTY ALL ON ITS OWN

5

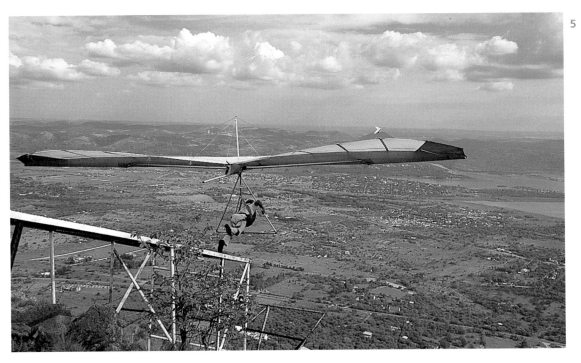

6

7

A prime leisure area for city-dwellers is Hartbeespoort Dam, in the foothills of the Magaliesberg. Crowded though it might be at times, there are some lovely corners where one can relax in peace. More intrepid sight-seers take to the air in hang-gliders launched from the backing hills (5), and curio vendors display their wares along the road (6). The dam entices yachting, boating and watersports enthusiasts (7&8), anglers, bird-watchers, ramblers and campers in their thousands over weekends.

8

1

A DRAMATIC DROP FROM THE EDGE OF THE HIGHVELD, A REGION OF
NATURAL WONDERS AND FORGOTTEN **GOLDFIELDS**

2

3

4

The high country. For sheer scenic beauty few parts of Africa can match the Mpumalanga Escarpment, and most especially the area cut through by the Blyde River and its majestic canyon (1). There are stunning views of the deep gorge, the distinctive buttresses known as the Three Rondavels (2) and the hot lowveld plain below the Escarpment – best seen from God's Window (3). Close by is an eye-catching fantasia of water-eroded rocks known as Bourke's Luck Potholes (4).

WONDROUS **WATERFALLS, COOL, CLEAR** MOUNTAIN POOLS
THAT LIE LIMPIDLY ALONG THE **RIVER** COURSES

5

6

7

8

The Escarpment is renowned for its many waterfalls, among them the Horseshoe (1), the Bridal Veil (2) and the Lisbon Falls (3), while the Mac-Mac Pools (4) tempt with a cooling swim. Pilgrim's Rest is a small nineteenth-century gold-mining town, lovingly preserved in its original condition. Its charms include the wares of roadside vendors (5), the old general dealer's (6), the miners' cottages (7), and the Royal Hotel pub (9). Visitors can watch the old-style extraction, or 'panning', of alluvial gold (8).

9

Named after the heavy siege-gun (1) used by the retreating Boers with devastating effect in the war of 1899–1902, is the scenic Long Tom Pass (3). Among the natural wonders of the countryside are the Sudwala Caves (2); other, less imposing attractions include some rather eccentric farm stalls (4) and the mampoer (5) – a powerful home brew – they sell.

6

7

8

9

South Africa's famed Blue Train, the ultimate in luxury travel, makes its way through eastern Mpumalanga (6), a region much favoured by fly-fishermen (7). The Badplaas Nature Reserve (8) and Nelspruit's Lowveld Botanical Garden (9) are other prime drawcards to the eastern end of the province.

93

1

THE **KRUGER**, PRINCE OF SOUTH AFRICA'S **GAME PARKS**, A VAST, **HEAT-HAZED EXPANSE** OF LOW-LYING BUSHVELD

The Kruger National Park, stretching across the eastern part of Mpumalanga and the Northern Province, is home to nearly 150 different kinds of mammal and to a splendid variety and number of birds. The sanctuary hosts some 5,000 visitors each day but manages, despite the massive human presence, to remain a pristine wilderness (1).

2

3

4

5

6

Among the Kruger's dazzling wildlife complement are the 'Big Five' so sought after by game-viewers. The quintet comprises the elusive leopard (2), the lion (3), the endangered black rhino and its white cousin (4), the mostly gentle but occasionally agitated elephant (5), and the African buffalo (6).

1

The Kruger Park is a game-viewer's paradise; options include the conducted drive (1&2) and the more intimate wilderness trail (3). However, visitors who simply make their way, to wait patiently at one of the many waterholes (4) are nearly always richly rewarded.

2

3

4

5

6

7

8

The Hippo Pools (5) are among the Kruger's
more popular viewing sites; other visitors prefer
to watch the animals from elevated comfort,
such as from the game hide at Bataleur (6).
Among the 500 or so bird species recorded in
the park are the white-breasted vulture (7)
and, in the lush riverine parts, the brown-
hooded kingfisher (8). The region is especially
renowned for its raptors; notables include
the spectacular fish eagle, the bateleur
and the secretary bird.

6

7

8

9

Visitors to the Kruger can choose from among more than 209 pleasant rest camps, some of them, like Skukuza, the 'capital' of the park (1,2,3&4), are big and busy. It is more like a thriving little town than a safari venue, boasting a huge reception and restaurant area (thought to be the world's largest thatched building), supermarket, bank, post office, police station and airfield. Olifants (5) enjoys a splendid position atop a high cliff; Shimuwini is small and intimate (6), Pretoriuskop (7) is the oldest camp; Bateleur (8) one of the quieter ones; and Punda Maria (9) the northernmost.

CENTURIES AGO, THE **LOWVELD** WAS HOME TO CULTURALLY ADVANCED **AFRICAN** COMMUNITIES

The interesting baobab tree (1) is a part of the diverse flora of the Kruger National Park. Curios are available not only from the rest camp shops, but also from local sellers (2). 'Transport riders' plied these fever-plagued lowveld plains in the early days of white settlement – among them author Percy FitzPatrick, who wrote stirring tales of adventure in the company of his dog Jock. This memorial to the faithful animal (3) lies within the park. Also of interest to visitors are the so-called 'Kruger Tablets' (4), and the Elephant Hall (5) at Letaba rest camp. A fair representation of the legacy of centuries-old African communities can be seen at the Albasini ruins (6) around Pretoriuskop, the ruins at Thulamela (7), and in the Masorini open-air museum (8). Letaba, like numerous rest camps in the park, offers some fine dining (9).

The Great North Road leads straight and true from Pretoria, across the tropic of Capricorn, to the tree-mantled Soutspansberg hills and Kipling's great, grey, greasy Limpopo. The land to the east of the highway, much of it Venda country, is remarkable for its scenic splendour, and for the customs and legends of its people. Its most striking natural feature is Lake Fundudzi (1), a sacred place wreathed in myth, lair of the python god of fertility. Not too far away are the ruins of Dzata (2), once the royal Venda village.

3

4

5

Many rural Venda still live in traditional 'rondavel' type homes (3). Rituals, such as the sinuous *domba* snake-dance, performed by young girls to mark their entry into womanhood (4), are still observed, and these Venda women (5) dress according to custom, although with some Western modifications.

1

2

3

4

5

The Northern Province is renowned for its curative mineral springs and the family resorts that have been developed around them, such as Warmbaths (1). Everywhere there are flowering trees and, less attractive but more intriguing, bizarre baobabs (2) that started life before the birth of Christ and have grown to immense proportions over the centuries. Between the highway and the Kruger National Park in the east lies a land of infinite variety and contrast: the lovely Magoebaskloof hills are clothed in pine forests (3), while much of the immensely fertile countryside is given over to subtropical fruits, nuts, cotton, coffee and to great tea plantations (4). The Waterberg (5) to the west is a region that is growing increasingly popular with those in search of African wilderness.

Although many people never go adventuring beyond the N1 Highway that slices through the Free State, it is a region that deserves more exploration. The eastern Free State is a fertile as well as scenically enchanting region, kind to the growers of wheat, fruit and golden sunflowers (1). By visual contrast the western plains are somewhat featureless, but here too the soil is rich, the windswept grasslands nurturing vast numbers of sheep and cattle. To the north is the Vaal River and its great dam (2).

A REGION OF **CONTRASTS**, FROM THE **DESOLATE** KAROO TO **FLAMBOYANT SUNFLOWER** FIELDS AND **RED-STONED** MOUNTAINS

The waters of the Vaal River and its dam are deep, and a perennial favourite with whitewater canoeists (3), fishermen (4) and power-boat enthusiasts (5). On the eastern shore of the giant reservoir is the resort village of Deneysville, home to a number of artists and crafters (6), and to the Lake Deneys Yacht Club (7).

FREE STATE

The eastern Free State is one of the country's chillier regions, with snow sometimes falling on the mountains in winter (1). It is scenically spectacular, rising in a series of often strangely weathered sandstone hills and cliffs that are at their most dramatic in the Golden Gate Highlands National Park (2,3&4). The flatter land, its soil deep and rich, is given over to crop-farming.

5

6

7

8

For the most part, life for the rural Sotho of the eastern Free State is conducted at an unhurried pace (5), and the old ways persist in the remoter parts. A little of the local culture can be seen at the Basotho Cultural Village (6). The surrounding countryside is a gentle lotion for the eyes (7); that of the high central plateau to the west (8) looks bleaker, but it has its own appeal, a beauty conferred by its big skies and far horizons.

FREE STATE

Among the country's most attractive villages is Clarens with its pretty little sandstone church (1). The village, nestled in the uplands of the eastern Free State, is a haven for a surprising number of artists of various kinds. These creative folk – painters, sculptors, potters, weavers, writers, photographers – have been drawn to the place by the tranquillity and the scenic splendour. Many of their homes are beautiful, filled with fine furniture, art, and craftwork; some house galleries and are open to the public. Colourful crafty shops are plentiful (3&4). The San have left their artistic imprint on the area too: many rock-faces are decorated with their paintings (2).

5

6

7

Set high on the great central plateau is Bloemfontein (5), once the capital of the Boer Republic of the Orange Free State, today the seat of the provincial government and South Africa's judicial capital. Notable among this quiet city's many stately buildings are the Fourth Raadsaal, or republican parliament (6) and the Old Residency (7), one-time home to the Boer republican presidents.

1

The great highland rampart that defines KwaZulu-Natal's western boundary is known as the Drakensberg ('Dragon Mountain'), an awesome sequence of often snow-capped peaks and buttresses, deep ravines, and precipitous cliffs. Among the many rivers that rise on the high plateau called Mont-aux-Sources is the Tugela (1&2); Mont-aux-Sources is the goal for many keen hikers (3). Below its towering splendour, in the foothills, lies the scenic Royal Natal National Park (4), one of its most enchanting features, the Cascades (5).

Dominating the northern heights of the Drakensberg is the distinctively straight-edged Amphitheatre (1&2). Notable birds of prey, here and elsewhere, include the bearded vulture, or lammergeier (3). To the south, the Injasuthi Buttress towers above the Giant's Castle area (4); both are magnets for the hiker.

4

THE DRAKENSBERG – TO CLIMBERS, THE **HEIGHTS** ARE A **CHALLENGE**;
TO EVERYONE ELSE, THEY ARE **GRAND** BEYOND DESCRIPTION

The Giant's Castle reserve, with its three rest camps (1, 3 & 4) and network of hiking trails, is part of the wider Drakensberg Park. It was originally created as a sanctuary for eland but now hosts a dozen or so different kinds of antelope. It is especially renowned, however, for its scenic grandeur, its flora (2) (most of the Berg's 800 or so species of flowering plant are found here) and for its 'galleries' of superb San rock art.

The Cathedral Peak area of the central Drakensberg is a splendid complex of massifs and pinnacles (5), most of which bear strikingly descriptive names – the Bell, the Pyramid, the Organ Pipes, the Mitre, the Chessmen among them. Cathedral Peak itself, rising 3,004 metres above sea level, is a strenuous full-day climb. In the hills below you'll find exquisite Zulu basketry on sale (6) and the Cathedral Peak Hotel (7).

Nestled in the lower hills of the southern Drakensberg is the scenically pleasant Loteni Nature Reserve (1&2). Resort hotels offer all the outdoor leisure amenities, including golf; this immaculate green (3) is part of the Glengary Country Club course. Loteni is one of a scatter of sanctuaries that entice the rambler (4), the botanist and the fly-fisherman.

Among formally protected areas in the southern Drakensberg is the Kamberg reserve (5), which boasts 13 kilometres of trout-stocked water (6). The only route that breaches the entire 250-kilometre length of the range is that over the steep and tortuous Sani Pass, in the southern section. The name refers to the ancient San, or Bushmen, of the region, whose rock art still decorates many of its cave and cliff walls (7). A tranquil Zulu village graces the plains below the high Drakensberg (8).

119

For much of the nineteenth century KwaZulu-Natal was a vast battleground over which Zulu, Boer and Briton fought for possession of the land. Reminders of that violent past include the memorials on the field of Isandlwana, where the Zulu army wiped out a 1,000-plus British force in 1879 (1&2), gravestones at Fort Pearson (3), and the monument at Spioenkop (4), perhaps the most savage battle of the Anglo-Boer War.

5

Among other memorials to the fallen in the Anglo-Boer War are those at Elandslaagte (5&6). The site of the famous Rorke's Drift engagement between the British and the Zulu looks much as it did in 1879 (7). Ten thousand Zulu soldiers died in the battle fought at Blood River in 1838. These bronze replicas of the laagered Boer ox-wagons honour the victors (8).

6

7

BOER, BRITON AND ZULU PLAYED OUT THEIR **BLOODY DRAMAS** ON THE PLAINS

8

Sightseeing by hot-air balloon is an exhilarating option (1) for seeing the Midlands. A prime recreational area is the Midmar Dam and nature reserve (2). Cottage industries are a regional feature; pictured are a woman sorting weaving yarn (3), handwoven goods at Shuttleworth (4) and a colourful local building (5).

6

9

7

10

8

Visitors can explore the gentle countryside north of Pietermaritzburg via the Midlands Meander, a route that takes in the art studios, early and rather charmingly modest settler homes (6), craft workshops, small factories, their retail outlets (7), country hotels and lodges (8&9), and much else. The region is also renowned for its fishing opportunities (10).

K W A Z U L U - N A T A L

To the east of the Midlands, and running down almost to the sea, is the majestic Valley of a Thousand Hills (1). Howick is a friendly, attractive little Midlands town, not far from Pietermaritzburg. For the most part, though, visitors know it for its position on the route taken by the Umgeni steam train (2), and for the charms of its surrounds, among which are the Howick Falls (3&4).

5

6

7

8

In visual terms Pietermaritzburg, an hour's drive inland from Durban, is a somewhat Victorian place, the colonial legacy evident in the stately lines of its City Hall (5) and in various monuments to Queen Victoria (6). The great Mahatma Gandhi, who had early associations with the region, is also honoured (7). The city is graced with the filigreed elegance of the pavilion and bandstand at Alexandra Park (8).

1

2

DURBAN BAY IS AFRICA'S FINEST NATURAL HARBOUR,
THE PORT AMONG THE HEMISPHERE'S BUSIEST

3

4

Durban, the country's premier holiday playground and port city, grew up around one of the southern hemisphere's finest natural harbours. It now includes a yacht basin that hosts a myriad small leisure craft (1), and among the prominent features of its docks (2) are the huge sugar terminal buildings (3). Most visitors, though, beat a path to the city's Golden Mile (4,5&6), a six-kilometre stretch of glittering ocean frontage, of sand and surfing rollers, piers, pavilions and pools, malls and markets, lawns, fountains, graceful walkways, hotels, restaurants and exuberant nightspots.

5

6

Focal point of Durban's arts scene is the Bartle Arts (or Bat) Centre (1), a complex of innovative workshops and studios. Among the city's more relaxing venues are its waterfront bistros (2). Zulu creativity of a different kind can be seen in the elaborate ornamentation of the ricksha pullers (3) and in street displays (4) of handcrafted ceramics and beadwork.

Playtime on the Golden Mile. Everyone can enjoy the performing dolphins at Sea World (5), a renowned marine research complex that embraces, among much else, huge shark tanks and shows that also feature seals and penguins. For shoppers, there's The Wheel (6), a multi-themed mall of some 150 speciality outlets, restaurants, bars and cinemas, while youngsters can have fun at the fascinating Minitown (7) or in the pools of Waterworld (8&9).

129

Contrast in styles. Durban's neo-Baroque City Hall (1), built in the high summer of Edwardian imperial confidence, dominates the central district. The golden-domed Jumma Musjid mosque (2), the southern hemisphere's biggest place of worship, serves the metropolis's Muslim community.

Make your way west of Durban city centre and you'll find yourself in an appealingly exotic world of saris, spices and the semi-tonal sounds of the Orient (3&4). This is the Indian trading area; many of the shopkeepers and their customers trace their ancestry to the labourers who arrived, on contract, from the 1860s onwards. Almost as colourful are the Workshop mall (5), the city's pavement displays of ingredients for traditional medicinal cures (6) and the produce market (7).

A large segment of Durban's Indian population follows the Hindu faith; the religion's most prominent place of worship is the Hare Krishna Temple of Understanding (1&2) in Chatsworth, about 20 minutes' drive from the city centre. The building is an eye-catching mix of Eastern and Western styles, reflecting the cross-cultural nature of the movement – the International Society of Krishna Consciousness, a Hindu society, was born centuries ago but has, in fairly recent times, extended its influence and following well beyond India. Durban and its surrounds boast some splendid shopping malls, notable among which is The Pavilion (3).

4

5

6

7

Garlanded Hindu bridal couples (4) and Hindu shrines (6) lend dignity and brightness to the Durban scene. Recommended for more tranquil excursions are the Japanese Gardens in Virginia (5), and the Umgeni River Bird Park, a quiet place of pools, waterfalls and enormous walk-through aviaries built into the cliff-face. The aviaries are filled with macaws (7) and a myriad other tropical species.

K W A Z U L U · N A T A L

Across the Umgeni River to the north of Durban lies the upmarket resort and residential centre of Umhlanga Rocks (1), noted for its luxury hotels, apartment complexes, stylish shops and restaurants – and for the nearby headquarters of the Natal Sharks Board, which welcomes visitors (tours and demonstrations are laid on). Beyond is the tropically lush Dolphin Coast, its secluded bays, golden beaches and attractive clusters of holiday homes. Notable among the many little seaboard venues are Ballito (2) and Shaka's Rock (3).

A **BALMY CLIMATE**, AND WIDE **GOLDEN BEACHES** LAPPED BY THE **WARM WATERS** OF THE INDIAN OCEAN

The shoreline to the south of Durban – the Sunshine and Hibiscus coasts – is a holidaymaker's paradise, its enduring assets a balmy subtropical climate, wide expanses of beach lapped by the warm blue Indian Ocean. Inland is the Oribi Gorge (4), a spectacular canyon that cuts through a rugged countryside of hill and deep valley, forest, stream and waterfall. The coast hides a score and more sunlit towns, villages and hamlets. Among the bigger and better known of the seaside centres are Margate (5) and Scottburgh (7). Subtropical fruit and vegetables for sale (6) add further colour to the already lush landscape, with its luxuriant hinterland greened by great sugarcane plantations (8).

Zululand, historic heartland of the Zulu nation, lies to the north of the Tugela River. It's a luxuriant part of the country, hot, humid, endowed with a distinctive human fabric and, in its famed game sanctuaries, an unparalleled array of wildlife. Major conservation areas include the Hluhluwe-Umfolozi Park, home to the endangered rhino (1) and much else. Here, wilderness hikers examine a rhino midden (2). Nearest centre to the park (3) is the village of Hluhluwe (pronounced 'shloo-shloo-ee').

4

5

The Hluhluwe-Umfolozi Park, which combines two of Africa's oldest game sanctuaries, ranks among the aristocrats of the conservation world. Game-viewers overnight on extended wilderness trails (4); others are accommodated at the Hilltop rest camp (5). The park's wooded hills and grasslands are a haven for the 'Big Five' (lion, leopard, rhino, elephant, buffalo), cheetah, giraffe (6) and much else.

6

Mkuzi Game Reserve, part of the Greater St Lucia Wetland Park, is renowned for its birdlife, much of which congregates at the Nsumu Pan. Here there are ghostly fever trees, crocodiles and hippos, and a wealth of water-related birds that can be observed in comfort from a strategically sited hide (1). The larger animals gather at various waterholes (2); for visitors, there's the cosy, tented Nhlonhela bush camp (3). Farther to the west, in the Pongolo River area, lies the equally well-endowed Itala Game Reserve (4).

5

6

The Itala sanctuary, upgraded and re-stocked in fairly recent times, offers splendid game-viewing along its network of roads (5). Some 75 different kinds of mammal inhabit its hilly grasslands and bushveld. In the far north, on the Pongolo floodplain, is the exquisite little Ndumo Game Reserve, notable for the richness of its riverine life, its giant sycamore fig trees (6) and the wealth of its wildlife (7). Ndumo is also home to around 420 species of bird.

7

The Greater St Lucia Wetland Park, which sprawls over much of KwaZulu-Natal's tropical northern spaces and was recently elevated to the status of World Heritage Site, is a complex of lake, swamp, forest, grassland, high dune and marine wilderness. Visitor amenities include lake cruises and boats for hire (1). Lake St Lucia itself hosts crocodiles, hippos (2) and flocks of flamingos. Accommodation is in charming little lake-side camps (3).

Wildlife to be seen around the lake and elsewhere includes the white pelican (4), the Nile crocodile, a female of which is seen here with her eggs (5), the lily-trotting African jacana (6), and the dainty little red duiker (7). The St Lucia marine sanctuary extends northwards from Cape Vidal (8) to Sodwana Bay; prominent features are lofty, vegetated dunes, pristine stretches of beach and, offshore, the world's southernmost coral reefs.

KWAZULU-NATAL

Hikers explore the dunes of St Lucia's Tewate Wilderness Area (1). Basketware is made locally and sold along the main routes of the region (2). The seaboard here is a magnet for giant sea-turtles that come to lay their eggs on the beaches. These loggerhead hatchlings (3), and those of the leatherbacks (4), struggle for survival against ghost crabs and other predators on their hazardous way back to the sea. Scuba-divers explore the offshore waters (5); Thonga villagers fish the northern lakes in the manner of their forefathers (6), using fish traps.

5

MAPUTALAND – A SUBTROPICAL **PARADISE** OF WILD WETLANDS AND **DUNES**, ITS SEA A TREASURY OF **COLOURFUL LIFE**

6

KWAZULU-NATAL

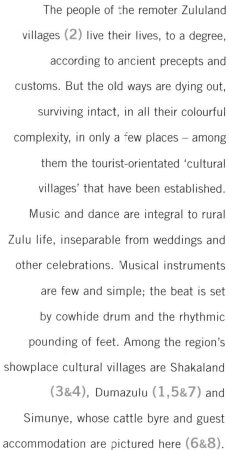

The people of the remoter Zululand villages (2) live their lives, to a degree, according to ancient precepts and customs. But the old ways are dying out, surviving intact, in all their colourful complexity, in only a few places – among them the tourist-orientated 'cultural villages' that have been established. Music and dance are integral to rural Zulu life, inseparable from weddings and other celebrations. Musical instruments are few and simple; the beat is set by cowhide drum and the rhythmic pounding of feet. Among the region's showplace cultural villages are Shakaland (3&4), Dumazulu (1,5&7) and Simunye, whose cattle byre and guest accommodation are pictured here (6&8).

5

6

7

8

1

THE **WILD COAST**, A MATCHLESS, 280-KILOMETRE STRETCH OF UNSPOILT **SUBTROPICAL WILDERNESS**

2

3

4

5

6

7

The Eastern Cape's Wild Coast, which runs from a point north of East London to KwaZulu-Natal, is famed for its sandy bays, its lagoons, estuaries, cliffs and rocky reefs (1). It is popular with hikers, such as these near Mazeppa Bay (2). However, this rural school (3) shows the poverty-stricken reality behind the façade. Pictured here, women selling their crafts (4), saltwater fly-fishing at the Kwelera River mouth (5), locals collecting mussels from the shoreline rocks (6), and hikers crossing a river estuary (7).

EASTERN CAPE

The Wild Coast has earned its name: its seaboard and offshore waters are treacherous – gales, currents and reefs have wrecked scores of ships over the centuries, including the *Jacaranda* (1). Numerous rivers flow into the sea along this daunting coastline, and offer enticing boating opportunities (2). Double Mouth (3) is one of many beautiful estuaries.

4

5

6

7

The region south-west of East London is scenically superb. Inland is the entrancing Hogsback area (4,5&6) where hikers and ramblers, guided by trail signs (7) along the country lanes and fern-fringed woodland paths, enjoy breathtaking vistas of the Amatola Mountains (8).

8

149

Lying to the north of the Amatolas are the uplands of the Katberg and the fertile valley of the Kat River (1). The Eastern Cape, one of the country's poorer but also among its most visually varied and scenic regions, is the historic home of the Xhosa people. The Xhosa are of Nguni stock and comprise numerous, culturally distinct groupings.

4

5

6

According to rural Xhosa custom, the men and boys take care of the cattle (2) – traditionally a sign of wealth. Rural Xhosa women, those who follow the time-honoured ways, are known for their fine beadwork and colourful garments. Women are responsible for food preparation (3) and farming. Many country homes are still built to the traditional 'rondavel' design, while others conform to modern conventions (4). Xhosa youths whiten their bodies in preparation for lengthy initiation rites (5) that will usher them into manhood. Circumcision remains a painful and sometimes hazardous part of the process. Here a wedding group (6) gathers to celebrate.

EASTERN CAPE

East London, the country's only major river-port, is a pleasant little city that caters for the quieter holidaymaker. The place is noted for its museum, for the spacious waters of the Buffalo estuary (1), and for its three broad beaches. Pictured are the city hall (2), scuba-divers on a day out (3) and the indigenous strelitzia plant (4), an unusual local specimen. Nahoon Beach (5) is an especially fine surfing spot.

6

Port Elizabeth is the economic hub of the Eastern Cape, and the country's headquarters for motor manufacturing and related industries. It's also known, deservedly, as the 'friendly city'. A magnificent beachfront (6&7) and pleasant colonial architecture that includes the terrace houses along Donkin Street (8) are among its assets. Market traders (9) are part of the exuberant occasion of the annual National Arts Festival held in graceful Grahamstown, some way inland (10).

7

8

9

10

EASTERN CAPE

The Eastern Cape, though well south of classic bushveld big-game country, sustains a surprising variety of wildlife havens. Foremost is the Addo Elephant National Park (1&3), home to a growing remnant of the Cape's once-great elephant herds. Dung beetles (2), the 'vacuum cleaners of the veld', are among the myriad other life forms, large and small, that thrive here. Private sanctuaries include the beautifully appointed, well-stocked Shamwari Reserve (4&5).

6

Much of the rugged Baviaanskloof ('baboon's ravine') area (6) is protected wilderness, a stunningly beautiful haven to rare plants and some 58 mammal species, including the formerly endangered Cape mountain zebra. Many locals work on farms in the Willowmore district (7) where aloes are harvested for the syrup-like substance they yield (8,9&10).

7

8

9

10

A REGION OF **FAR HORIZONS** AND OF **VOLCANIC OUTCROPS**
WEATHERED INTO **STARK**, OFTEN BIZARRE SHAPES

4

5

The north-western part of the Eastern Cape is occupied by the lonely wastes of the Great Karoo, its most spectacular feature the well-named Valley of Desolation (1). The valley overlooks Graaff-Reinet, a quiet and charming old town with an array of historic buildings that includes the Dutch Reformed church (2). Karoo children make and sell models of the myriad windmills that draw life-giving water from below the arid surface of the land (3&4). Among the area's more eccentric venues is the Owl House in the timeless hamlet of Nieu-Bethesda: here, local sculptor Helen Martins dreamed and delved into the land of fantasy (5&6). The Mountain Zebra National Park (7) is a haven for the endangered Cape mountain zebra (8).

6

7

8

At the eastern end of the Garden Route is Storms River with its attractive rest camp of simple bungalows (1). Notable are an exquisite waterfall (2) reached on the first day of the Otter Trail hike, the Paul Sauer Bridge (3), rising a dizzy 140 metres above the racing river, the wondrous explosions of water against 'Skietklip' ('shooting rock') (4), and the suspension bridge at the river mouth (5). Running westwards for 80 kilometres is the Tsitsikamma National Park, sanctuary for forest, ferns, heath, wild orchids and lilies; for baboon, bushbuck, Cape clawless otter (6), and for nearly 300 kinds of bird. The park is also a marine reserve where rock pools teem with colourful life, whales and dolphins sport offshore and the Storms River surges through a deep gorge into the Indian Ocean (7).

5

6

7

Running through the Tsitsikamma park is the Otter Trail. It leads through an entrancing countryside of natural forest, streams and waterfalls, and along a coast of beaches, high cliffs and little coves (1). It is a leisurely hike, allowing time to enjoy the vistas, study the plant, animal and birdlife, take a dip in the sea, or snorkel in the tidal pools. The trail ends at Nature's Valley, a small village in a setting of tree-mantled mountain, lagoon and sea (2). Further down the coast is the beautiful Salt River estuary (3). Denizens of the forest depths include the little vervet monkey (4).

Probably the most fashionable of the Garden Route's seaside towns is Plettenberg Bay, a sophisticated resort centre with fine beaches and hotels in spectacular surrounds (5). The area enjoys an average 320 days of unbroken sunshine a year. To the south-west of town lies the Robberg Peninsula, a nature and marine reserve (6). Just along the coast, near the Keurbooms River mouth, is the distinctive Cathedral Rock (7), while delicate 'pansy shells' (8) are prized finds along the beaches.

'THIS LAND, **THE GIFT OF GOD**' – A FITTING TESTAMENT TO THE
BEAUTY OF **LAGOON** AND HILL-AND-FOREST COUNTRYSIDE

There are many fine beaches along this stretch of coast such as Noetzie (1). Knysna's motto, 'This land, the gift of God', is a fitting testament to the charm of the town, its famed lagoon and the surrounding hill-and-forest countryside with their elusive but colourful birds, among them the Knysna lourie (2). The lagoon is a limpid, 17-kilometre-long expanse of water, its sea entrance guarded by two sandstone cliffs known as The Heads (3); among its enticements are a little waterfront (5), pleasure cruises (6), plenty of opportunities for canoeing, waterskiing, fishing, rambling – and for just relaxing in the sunshine (7). Worth visiting is the pleasing little Norman-style church at Belvidere (4). The indigenous forests of the area are renowned for their giant yellowwood trees (8).

1

2

3

The dense evergreen hardwood forests around Knysna (1) can be explored via a network of trails. This farmstall (2) is named for the six-hour Elephant Walk, a reference to the remnants of the great herds of Cape elephants that once sought sanctuary in the forest depths. Knysna, Wilderness to the west, and the inland town of George are linked by the 'Outeniqua Choo-Tjoe', a narrow-gauge railway along which a vintage Class 24 steam train, here seen crossing the Kaaimans River estuary (3), puffs its way each day. Between Knysna and the village of Wilderness (4) is the 'Lake District'. Here lie half-a-dozen beautiful stretches of water, all different in character, each supporting a fascinating variety of fish, aquatic plants and birds. For visitors, there are excellent hotels and comfortable rest camps (5) and, along the coast, beaches that beckon the bather and sun-worshipper. This one (6) fringes Victoria Bay.

The town of George, set on a pleasant plain below the wooded heights of the Outeniqua Mountains, is the 'capital' of the Garden Route. The luxurious Fancourt Country Club, which boasts one of the southern hemisphere's finest golf courses (1), was chosen to host the 2002 President's Cup, which pits the US's top players against the best of the world's rest. Among the area's considerable charms is George's elegant Dutch Reformed church (2), and the seaside resort of Herold's Bay to the south (3).

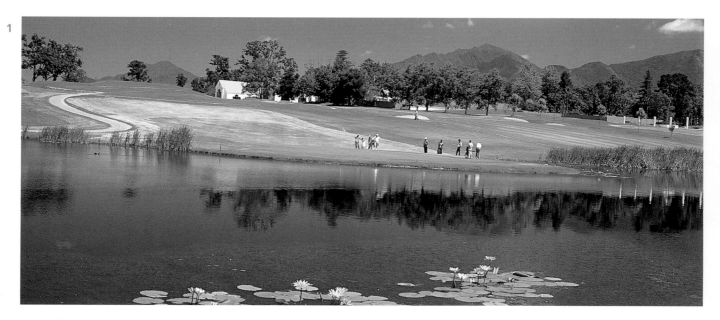

At the western end of the Garden Route is Mossel Bay, where Portuguese navigator Bartholomeu Dias, during his sterling attempt to chart the sea lane between Europe and India, stepped ashore in 1487. The event can be relived in the Dias Museum (4). The town caters handsomely for the holidaymaker, and its harbour is bright with luxury leisure craft (5). Mossel Bay (6), once a sleepy little seaside village of limewashed homes (7), has grown considerably since the discovery of offshore oilfields and is now a busy industrial and commercial centre.

To the north of the Garden Route, beyond the coastal rampart, lies a dry but richly fertile plain called the Little (or 'Klein') Karoo, a region separated from the Karoo proper by the spectacular, sometimes snow-clad and always beautiful heights of the Swartberg range (1&2).

The biggest town in the Little Karoo is Oudtshoorn, which flourished and grew on the back of a late-Victorian and Edwardian fashion industry and its insatiable appetite for ostrich feathers. Those who farmed the big birds, and others who traded in their products, made enormous fortunes. The area has much to offer today's visitor: ostrich show-farms (3); the ostentatious homes built by 'ostrich barons' and known as 'feather palaces' (4); the Cango Cave complex, ranked as one of the country's great natural wonders (5); and the Cango Crocodile Ranch and Cheetahland (6).

Orange-flowered aloes lend brave splashes of colour to the plains of the largely featureless semi-desert that is the Great Karoo (1). The region's 'capital' is Beaufort West, its most charming centre Matjiesfontein, a perfectly preserved Victorian village whose centrepiece is the Lord Milner Hotel (2). Close to Beaufort West lies the Karoo National Park (3), a treasure-house of aeons-old fossils (4), among them those of the massive reptiles known as the 'fearful heads', and home to springbok (5) and a variety of other dryland-adapted animals. Here and there, the monotony of the Karoon is relieved by rocky hills, like those known as the Three Sisters (6).

3

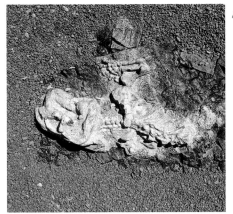

4

5

THE **GREAT KAROO** – A VAST SEMI-DESERT OF **TREELESS TERRAIN** AND LONELY HOMESTEADS

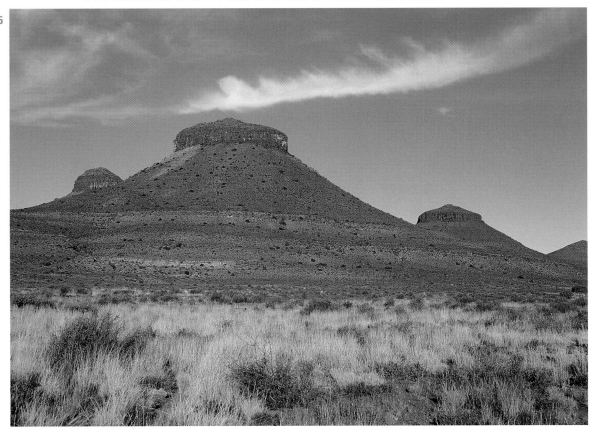

6

1

2

3

4

5

6

Across the Hottentots Holland Range east of Cape Town stretches the Overberg, an attractively scenic and immensely fertile region. Still Bay (1) has a charming little harbour; Malgas boasts the country's only surviving vehicle pont (2); Swellendam, biggest of the inland towns, retains much of its historic past, including the drostdy building (3). The fertile farming region (5) is cut through by the Breede River (4) which forms a boundary for the Bontebok National Park (6). The Overberg is famed for its springtime wild flowers (7), pleasant countryside, and a seaboard of infinite beauty and variety. In the Langeberg region, just over the mountains from Swellendam, Montagu (9) is distinguished by its surrounding vineyards and nearby mineral springs; Ashton by its thorougbred horses and dried-fruit industry (8).

7

8

9

1

2

3

4

5

A venerable lighthouse and commemorative cairn **(1&2)** greet visitors to Cape Agulhas, the most southerly point of Africa. Nearby Arniston, named after an especially tragic 19th-century shipwreck, is one of the region's more charming fishing villages **(3,5&6)**. Farther along the coast to the north-east sprawls the De Hoop Nature Reserve, a place of rolling vegetated dunes and home to black oystercatchers **(4)** and around 1,500 species of fragile 'fynbos' plants, including many kinds of pincushions **(8)**. The sanctuary is much favoured by mountain-bikers **(7)** and strollers **(9)**.

Hermanus (1), on the south coast, offers some of the world's best whale-watching. It stages the annual Whale Festival, is known for its market (2), and boasts what is thought to be the world's first and only whale-crier (3), who indicates the whereabouts of the great marine mammals, most of them 60-ton southern rights (4).

The town is attractively set between mountain and sea; prime observation sites for avid whale-watchers are the backing cliffs and coastal rocks **(5&9)**. Southern rights make their way close inshore to breed and calve from mid-winter to early summer. The Old Harbour **(6&7)** is now part of a museum complex, and the mountains behind Hermanus are popular with hang- and paragliders **(8)**.

THE ATLANTIC CAN BE GENTLE, BUT IS NOT ALWAYS SO – MANY SHIPS HAVE FOUNDERED ON ITS SHORES

From Hermanus, the coastal road westwards leads you along along the scenically memorable shoreline of False Bay (1) after passing through Betty's Bay, notable for its botanical garden (2), leading towards the busier beaches of Gordon's Bay and Strand.

3

4

Towards the eastern end of False Bay, and part of the Cape Town metropolitan area, is the pleasing seaside village of Gordon's Bay (3&4) and the next-door, larger towns of Strand (5) and Somerset West. Among the area's prime attractions are the forested Helderberg Nature Reserve and Vergelegen, a splendid Cape Dutch homestead and wine farm that began life in 1701 (6).

5

6

THE MOUNTAIN, RISING ABOVE THE CITY OF CAPE TOWN, IS AMONG THE WORLD'S BEST-KNOWN LANDMARKS

Table Mountain (1), among the world's most familiar landmarks, rises in all its majesty above Cape Town and the waters of Table Bay. Visitors ascend the heights by cable-car; fine views of sea, city and the flanking Lion's Head peak (2) unfold both on the way up and from the summit (3). Neighbouring Signal Hill hosts the noonday gun (4) and one of several Cape Town kramats, or Muslim shrines (6). Table Mountain, a nature reserve, provides spectacular climbing opportunities (5), and is a haven to dassies (hyraxes) (7) and delicate little disas (8).

3

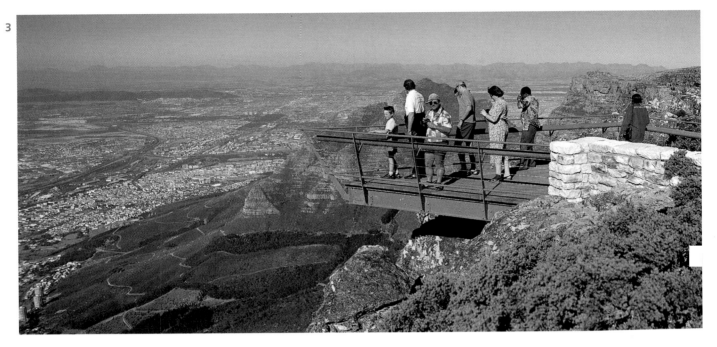

4

5

6

7

8

181

Open-air markets bring colour and animation to Cape Town's thoroughfares. In the surrounding streets weary shoppers can enjoy the sunshine outside any one of many restaurants (1). Practical, down-to-earth goods are sold on the stalls on the Grand Parade, which flanks the elegantly ornate City Hall (2). Among the biggest and busiest markets is that in cobbled Greenmarket Square (3), a magnet for trendy bargain-hunters. City flower-sellers brighten the streets with their blooms at knock-down prices (4).

5

6

7

8

9

Cape Town is one of the few South African cities that can comfortably be explored on foot; strollers favour old-fashioned Long Street (5) and enjoy the cheeky little squirrels (6) on Government Avenue (7). Among other sightseeing venues are the ill-fated but hopefully soon to be rejuvenated District Six (8) and the Castle, completed in 1676 and now the country's oldest occupied building (9).

VIBRANT BO-KAAP, WHERE MANY FREED SLAVES FIRST MADE THEIR HOMES, ON THE PICTURESQUE SLOPES OF SIGNAL HILL

The charming inner suburb of Bo-Kaap, also known as the Malay Quarter (1&3), is the historic home to part of Cape Town's Islamic community. The city's coloured folk have a lively musical culture that, though it draws on the minstrel traditions of the American Deep South, is distinctive to the Cape (2).

4

5

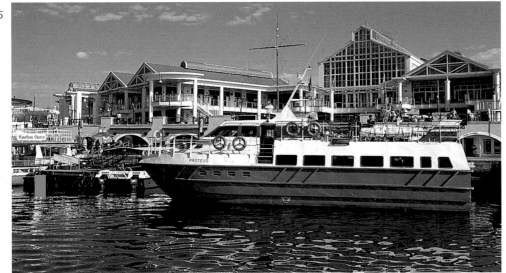

6

7

Cape Town's biggest drawcard is probably the Victoria & Alfred Waterfront (4,5&6), an ongoing harbour redevelopment that draws its inspiration from hugely successful dockside 'humanization' schemes in San Francisco, Boston, Sydney and elsewhere, but which has a personality very much its own. Old buildings have been converted, new ones constructed to house upmarket emporiums and speciality shops, markets and malls, restaurants, bistros and bars. The two historic dock basins are used by working boats as well as leisure craft, and are the hangout of scores of seagulls (7).

1

2

4

3

Adding to the Waterfront's (1) eclectic attractions are open-air shows (2), street buskers and mime artists (3) and the superb Two Oceans Aquarium (4).

5

6

7

8

Robben island (7) has served as a place of incarceration for centuries – criminals, the politically suspect, lunatics and lepers have been among its guests – but is now best known as a high-security prison (5) for opponents of the late apartheid regime. Nelson Mandela was its most famous inmate, and his cell (6) on the Island can be visited. Also pictured is the 'leper church' (8). A dockside ferry from the Waterfront takes you to the island's little harbour (9).

9

1

2

3

Sun, sea and sand. The first stretch of the Cape Peninsula's western shoreline is ruggedly rocky for the most part. Sea Point, close to the city, is graced by a pleasant promenade (1); Green Point's veteran lighthouse (2) is both a landmark and a national monument. Although the waters are usually too chilly for comfortable bathing, there are some lovely expanses of beach, notably along the trendy frontages of Clifton (3) and Camps Bay (4), where restaurants offer sea views as well as a culinary treat (5). The boulder-framed beach at Llandudno (6&7) farther down the Peninsula is another favourite.

1

2

3

4

Jewel of the Peninsula's western coast is Hout Bay (1), a fishing harbour and rather affluent residential area that huddles beneath wooded mountains. Salt-stained working boats (2&3) rub gunwales with status-affirming leisure craft in the picturesque harbour. Beyond, to the south, are the spacious sands of Noordhoek beach, long and lonely enough to offer riders a good gallop (4).

5

6

7

8

The Peninsula's far southern seaboard remains attractively wild, its coastal hamlets – such as Scarborough (5) and Smitswinkel Bay (7) – unpretentious, and tranquil in their isolation. The shores are rocky, seaweed-scented breecing grounds for tasty crayfish (6). The Cape of Good Hope Reserve is a treasure of fragile fynbos vegetation and home to baboons (8), known for their thieving ways. These particular animals are unique among non-human primates in their diet: they subsist largely on marine foods, which they garner at low tide.

191

Cape Point, off which the ghostly sailing ship *Flying Dutchman* has been observed from time to time over the centuries, is one of the region's finest viewsites which visitors can ascend by funicular (**1**). Nearby is a replica of the Dias Cross, or *padrão* (**2**), erected by the celebrated Portuguese navigator in 1488. Refreshments are served in the pleasant restaurant (**3**). Cape Point is the southernmost tip of the Peninsula, and from its cliffs one can see False Bay sweeping away to the mountains of the east (**4**), seabirds wheeling in the sky, whales and dolphins playing in the waters far below.

5

Close to Simon's Town, on the Peninsula's eastern, or False Bay seaboard, is Boulders beach, home to one of two mainland colonies of African penguin (5). Simon's Town has featured prominently in the naval annals; a stroll along its main street (7) offers a glimpse of its past. In Jubilee Square stands a statue of Just Nuisance (6), a much-loved dog who befriended British servicemen during the Second World War.

6

7

1

2

3

4

The eastern shoreline, gentler than the western, is lapped by the warm waters of False Bay, one of the country's major sailing, surfing and leisure areas. Among the attractive towns and villages that grace the coast are Fish Hoek (**1**); Kalk Bay (**2&3**), known for its fishing harbour, antique shops and eccentric characters (**4**); old-fashioned St James and its bathing huts (**6**), and Muizenberg, which boasts a magnificent beach (**5**).

A large part of the central plateau of the Peninsula is occupied by Constantia (1), an enchanting area of wooded slopes, secret valleys, vineyards (3), orchards – and of grand old homesteads which, together, comprise the Peninsula's wine route. The stateliest of the historic mansions is Groot Constantia (2), originally the home of the enterprising Dutch colonial governor Simon van der Stel (1639–1712) and now a prime tourist venue noted for its graceful architecture, its beautifully landscaped grounds, its wine museum and cellar. Wine tastings and sales are laid on; visitors have the choice of two fine restaurants.

4

5

6

7

KIRSTENBOSCH, **COLOURFUL HAVEN** FOR THE PLANTS OF ONE OF THE WORLD'S SIX GREAT **FLORAL KINGDOMS**

8

The world-famed Kirstenbosch Gardens (4), which decorate the eastern slopes of the Table Mountain range, nurture about half the country's 18,000 indigenous flowering plants, including a wealth of pincushions, proteas and ericas (5,6&7). Farther along the slopes is Rhodes Memorial (8), a temple-like structure that honours the nineteenth-century imperialist, tycoon, politician and controversial visionary Cecil John Rhodes.

1

2

3

The Cape metropole's northern suburbs have long been exiled from the tourism mainstream, but that is now changing, dramatically, with the recent development of major and enticing new venues for the shopper, the gambler and the leisure-bent visitor. Most spectacular among these is perhaps the vast Century City complex and its entertaining (and challenging) Ratanga Junction theme park (1&3). Pictured at left is the stomach-churning Cobra (2).

Century City and its upmarket Canal Walk (4&5), the southern hemisphere's largest shopping complex, embrace a glittering array of retail outlets together with restaurants, cinemas, waterfront, canals, an island, a small-craft harbour, wetland reserve and an innovative science centre. In nearby Goodwood is the GrandWest casino, entertainment and hotel enterprise (6,7&8).

Stellenbosch, in the fertile valley of the Eerste ('First') River north-east of Cape Town, began life in 1679, grew gracefully over the centuries and now serves as the charming hub of the Western Cape's winelands region (1). Historic venues include the Lanzarac Hotel (2), the wine cellars (3), the old general dealer's, Oom Samie se Winkel (4), and the quaint old homes on Dorp Street (5). Summer shows in the Oude Libertas Amphitheatre (6), strawberry picking (7&8), and the Spier wine farm (9) are other popular attractions.

5

6

7

8

9

Franschhoek (1&2), resting quietly in an enchanting valley to the east of Stellenbosch, was founded in the late 1600s by a small group of pious, and for the most part talented, French Huguenot (Protestant) exiles who had fled the religious troubles plaguing their homeland. Little remains of their language and culture, though their presence is reflected in many family names. The wine-farms (3) they carved from the land, and the homes they built add much to the beauty of the region. The Franschhoek Wine Cellar (4) is one of many places selling the fine wines of the district.

Near Franschhoek, picnics at Boschendal (5), a stately Cape Flemish homestead and wine farm, are a delight – as is the traditional buffet luncheon spread. The elegant little town of Franschhoek (6) itself is renowned for its antique shops, its *auberges* (inns) and cosy restaurants (7), most of them offering exquisite French cuisine. The Huguenot founders are commemorated by this graceful monument (8).

1

2

3

4

5

THE IMPRESSIVE **PAARL ROCK GLISTENS** ABOVE A **MYRIAD VINEYARDS**

Paarl (1&5), to the north of Franschhoek, is named after a trio of large, rounded, pearl-like rocks atop the overlooking mountain (2), boulders that glisten in the sunlit morning dew. Waterblommetjies, harvested on local dams (3) are cooked up with lamb into a delicious stew that is a regional speciality. The butterfly farm at Klapmuts (4) is one of many local attractions. This, too, is a splendid wine-farming area (7); leading attractions include the Laborie complex (6), Fairview (8) wine farm known for, among other things, its goat's cheese and 'goat tower', and La Concorde (9), headquarters of the giant KWV co-operative. The estates of the countryside around Paarl produce distinctive wines, and have highly individual personalities.

THE **RUGGED MOUNTAINS** OF THE **BOLAND** ARE SOMETIMES SNOW-CAPPED, THE **VALLEYS** BELOW FERTILE

Travellers on their way from Cape Town into the great interior pass beneath the strikingly scenic Hex River Mountains (1). Nearby is the pleasant town of Worcester, worth visiting for its open-air museum, its fine botanical garden (Karoo flora) and its farm stalls (2). The richly endowed Hex River Valley yields most of the country's late-maturing grapes (3).

Tulbagh and Ceres are two attractive country towns lying in the uplands. The town of Tulbagh (4) boasts the country's largest single group of historic buildings. To reach Ceres one must take the scenic route through Michell's Pass whose old toll-house still stands (5). Tulbagh produces good wines (6), but this is also fruit-growing country, many of the locals (7) working on fruit-farms. A number of major passes cut through the Boland's mountains, including Du Toit's Kloof Pass (8).

THE WESTERN SEABOARD, **LONG NEGLECTED** BY THE TOURIST,
IS **SLOWLY** OFFERING UP ITS **SECRETS** TO OUTSIDERS

4

5

6

7

South Africa's western seaboard, long neglected by business and the tourism industry, is now regarded as a growth area. Offshore islands are home to a myriad gannets and other seabirds (6); access to Dassen Island, described as 'one of the wonders of the naturalist's world', is restricted but it can be observed on boating excursions (1). Langebaan Lagoon's surrounds, conserved within the West Coast National Park, are famed for their springtime wild flowers, and the adjoining Postberg Nature Reserve for the occasional, rather bizarre, rock formation (2). The bird-rich lagoon (3) lies at the southern end of the sweeping Saldanha Bay. Close to Langebaan is the Mediterranean-style Club Mykonos resort complex (4&5). Biggest of the West Coast's urban centres is Saldanha (7), which boasts one of the country's finest natural harbours.

Among the pretty seaboard villages of the West Coast is Paternoster (1&2), its name – which means 'Our Father' – taken from a heartfelt prayer offered up by early shipwreck survivors. To the north of Saldanha is St Helena Bay, 'discovered' by Portuguese navigator Vasco da Gama in 1497 and now largely given over to commercial fishing. Crayfish, or rock lobster (3) are a lucrative catch, though to a diminishing extent as over-exploitation and poaching take their toll.

4

5

The coastal countryside (4), known as the sandveld, dons its most attractive mantle in the spring months. The waters off the western seaboard, cooled by the Benguela Current and rich in nutrients, nurture vast shoals of pilchards, anchovies and mackerel which, in turn, sustain the hardy fishermen of St Helena Bay (5). Farther up the coast is the town of Lambert's Bay and its celebrated Bird Island (6).

6

1

2

3

4

Inland from the western shores lies the Cedarberg, a grand upland wilderness of stark and often strangely weathered rock formations, of rugged peaks and ravines, forests, crystal-clear streams and waterfalls. Among the most famous of the striking rock formations are the Wolfberg Arch (1) and the Maltese Cross (2). Beyond the highlands to the east is the charmingly timeless village of Wuppertal (3), noted for the fine leather shoes it manufactures. Some of the area's caves and cliff faces are decorated with fine examples of ancient San (Bushman) rock art (4). The region is favoured by hikers (5) and campers (6).

213

The western coastal strip beyond the Olifants River is known as Namaqualand, a dry, sandy, scantily populated region that becomes more arid as one travels northwards towards the Gariep (formerly Orange) River. Forbidding though much of the countryside appears, however, it has its own beauty, most notably in the spring months when the wild flowers come into sudden, all-too-brief but glorious bloom, clothing the plains and hills in a riot of colour (1,2,4&5). A rare waterfall cascades near the inland village of Nieuwoudtville (3), while the Namaqualand coast is ruggedly rocky (6).

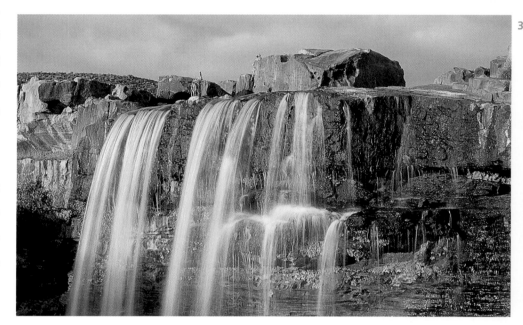

5

THE **DRY**, RATHER BLEAK **NAMAQUALAND** BECOMES A **WONDERLAND** OF WILD FLOWERS IN **SPRINGTIME**

6

5

6

8

Largest of Namaqualand's towns is Springbok; nearby lies the Goegap Nature Reserve, haven for the endearing little bat-eared fox (1), for a wealth of springtime wild flowers (2&4), for the weird koker-boom or 'quiver tree' (3), and for the angulate tortoise (7). Port Nolloth is a major fishing centre (6) on this coast. The Namaqualand region of the Northern Cape is home to a group of the Nama people (8), survivors of a distinct culture that was dominant in much of the country's western parts in the precolonial era. By tradition they are semi-nomadic herders, but most now live and work in permanent settlements. Here and there, though, one can still see the kind of home, originally built of reeds and somewhat temporary, that served their forebears so well (5).

7

1

THE **RICHTERSVELD** NATIONAL PARK – AN IMMENSE, **BONE-DRY MOUNTAIN DESERT** WILDERNESS

2

The Richtersveld National Park (1,2&4) is an immense, bone-dry mountain desert wilderness bounded in the north by a great curve in the Gariep River. The terrain is rugged, distinguished by bare, bleak hills, by jaggedly wind-sculpted rock formations and by bizarre 'halfmens' ('half-man') trees (2). By contrast the Gariep is flanked by refreshing greenery, the river attracting a steady stream of hikers, campers and canoeists (3&5). The Richtersveld is also a fascinating region for the botanist: fully one third of all the world's known mesembryanthemum species occur in the park.

1

At one stage on its long journey across the sand-and-scrub country-side of the Northern Cape, the Gariep River plunges through a massive, 18-kilometre-long canyon in a dramatic sequence of rapids and cascades. These are the Augrabies Falls (1), which finally breach the rim of the main gorge in a misty tumble of cataracts that, at peak flow, ranks as one of the world's six largest waterfalls. The gorge forms the centrepiece of the Augrabies Falls National Park, haven for rhino (2) and many other animals.

2

3

4

5

Straddling the Northern Cape's border with Botswana is the Kgalagadi Transfrontier Park, a vast and arid wilderness of Kalahari sand, scrub and ephemeral grassland that transcends national boundaries, and in doing so has become Africa's first 'peace park'. Dry and unforgiving though the land may look (4), it supports an astonishing variety and number of life forms, including the handsome, desert-adapted gemsbok (3) and the cheetah (5), swiftest of all mammals.

The Kgalagadi Transfrontier Park (1) is well geared to host visitors; largest of its three comfortable rest camps is Twee Rivieren (2), which means 'Two Rivers' and refers to twin watercourses that rarely flow. Their banks and dry beds, however, sustain acacias and other hardy trees. Among the park's residents are lions (3) that, in times of drought (which is the norm, not the exception, in this harsh wilderness), wander wide and far in their struggle for survival.

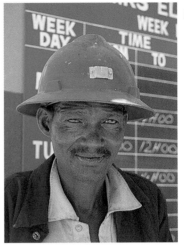

Kimberley, capital of the Northern Cape, began life in the 1870s, when fabulous deposits of diamonds were found in the area's kimberlite 'pipes'. The most renowned of the latter known as the 'Big Hole' (4): it produced around three tons of high-quality gems during its 45-year lifespan. Miners (5) still work Kimberley's diamond-rich earth; among local monuments is one that honours the brotherhood of diggers (6). The 'Big Hole' now forms the focus of the Kimberley Mine Museum, which includes a re-creation of part of the early town (7).